Complete Guide to

STAMPING

Complete Guide to
STAMPING

*Over 70 techniques with
20 original projects and 300 motifs*

WARRINGTON BOROUGH COUNCIL	
Cypher	27.06.04
761	£17.99

Alan D. Gear and Barry L. Freestone
with Sarah Beaman and Teresa Philpott

COLLINS & BROWN

First published in Great Britain in 2004 by
Collins & Brown Ltd
The Chrysalis Building
Bramley Road
London W10 6SP
An imprint of Chrysalis Books Group plc

Project Manager: Kate Haxell
Designer: Roger Daniels
Illustrator: Kuo Kang Chen
Indexer: Ann Parry

10 9 8 7 6 5 4 3 2 1

British Library Cataloguing-in-Publication Data:
A catalogue record for this title is available from the British Library.

ISBN 1–84340–104–5

Reproduction by Classicscan, Singapore
Printed and bound by Times Offset, Malaysia

CONTENTS

INTRODUCTION

One of the wonderful things about stamping is that it can produce great effects at many different levels. Even a complete beginner to the craft can easily create a decorative greeting card or a set of pretty stationery. You don't have to be skilled or artistic to get good results, since the stamps will do so much of the work for you.

However, as all stamping enthusiasts soon learn, once you master the basic techniques of stamping, a creative and exciting world awaits.

In our 25 years of working in the crafts forum, we have met stampers of all ages and abilities, each with one thing in common—they are passionate about their craft. And that's another thing about stamping—it's completely addictive. Most people, once they have pressed a stamp onto paper, never look back. They catch the bug and are soon stamping everything within reach.

With so much enthusiasm for the craft, it is not surprising that there are already many books on stamping. So why publish another one? The answer is simple: This book covers the whole spectrum of stamping, from choosing your first stamp, to original and creative embellishing techniques, to producing stunning projects for the home, for friends, and for you.

We have had great craftswomen working with us on this book. Sarah Beaman, a greeting card and scrapbooking aficionado, and Teresa Philpott, a stamping expert, have contributed ideas, projects, and their artistic and professional knowledge.

Divided into clear, easy-to-use chapters, this book will take the beginner to stamping through all the basic techniques needed to produce an effective stamped design.

Learn to make your own stamps, get professional advice on choosing ready-made stamps, and learn about the right media and methods of applying it. Discover which surfaces you can stamp onto, and how to place a stamp. All techniques are illustrated with clear step-by-step photographs and have detailed instructions, plus tips on how to make the most of a technique and achieve a perfect finish.

If you are a seasoned stamper and are already familiar with the basics—or once you have mastered them—you can move on to the creative techniques that turn a simple stamp into a work of art.

Six chapters look at coloring stamps, creative stamping techniques, working on fabric, embossing, three-dimensional stamping, and edible stamping. (If the last sounds surprising, turn to page 84 and see what you find.) All of these inspirational techniques—many developed especially for this book—will help you take your stamping skills to new heights.

At the back of the book are 300 motifs from which you can make your own stamps to use with any of the techniques illustrated. The only thing left to say is, Happy stamping!

Alan D. Gear
and
Barry L. Freestone

EQUIPMENT

You don't need much equipment to start stamping—stamps, inks and something to stamp onto will get you going. As you develop your skills, you will want to invest in more materials, but most of those will be new stamps and ink colors. Turn to page 28 for more advice on choosing stamps, and to page 32 for information on the different types of inks available, and how to use them.

There are other items you may wish to buy depending on what you want to stamp onto: Pages 38–45 will give you more information on stamping on different surfaces.

You will also want to decorate your stamps, but read through the technique you are interested in and then buy what you need, since decorative materials can be expensive and you won't use all of them at once. Build up a collection of materials and eventually you will have everything you need.

It is always best to have a room set aside for your craft projects so that you can leave work in progress out without its being damaged. If this is impossible, you will need to organize your equipment properly to keep it in good condition, and allow you to find what you need. There are many types of bags and racks available from craft stores to help you organize everything. Before choosing a storage system assess them carefully. Think about the equipment you have now and what items you may be buying in the future.

Shown on these pages are the basic items that it is worth investing in when you first start stamping.

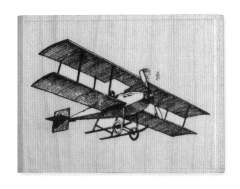

The most essential thing for any stamper is, of course, a stamp. Shown above are the back and stamping surface of a wooden stamp. These can be expensive, but buy the best you can afford, as you need them

and your collection will soon grow. Turn to pages 28–31 for more information on stamps, and to pages 12–27 for instructions on making your own when you just can't find the image you want for a project.

Foam stamps are inexpensive and are perfect for children to use. Turn to page 30 for more information.

Rainbow stamps are available in a wide range of colors, not just the traditional rainbow stripes. They offer an instant way of making a stamped image more decorative and are useful for detailing.

Tiny stamp pads are inexpensive and come in a wide range of colors.

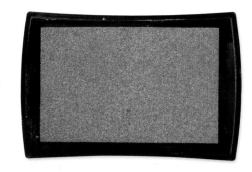

Pigment pads have a firm felt ink pad and the colors are permanent on most surfaces. Page 33 offers more advice on the different types of ink pads available and on how best to use them.

Foam pads are the most popular type of ink pad. They come in an enormous range of colors, including the metallic finish shown here.

Always use a soft pencil in conjunction with stamping so that you can easily rub out any marks.

A wide, medium-bristle paintbrush is the best type for applying paint to a stamp (see page 34 for instructions). A fine paintbrush is useful for coloring in a stamp (see page 55).

A craft knife is an essential tool for most crafters, and stampers are no exception. Use it in conjunction with a steel ruler to cut out stamped panels or trim cards. Buy a knife with a retractable blade and slide it away when you are not using it.

Buy a good-quality pair of scissors with sharp points for cutting out stamped designs.

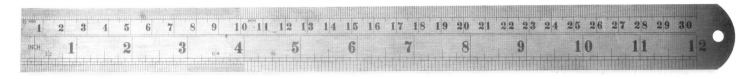

Choose a steel ruler with the measurement system you prefer; though some rulers do show both metric and imperial markings.

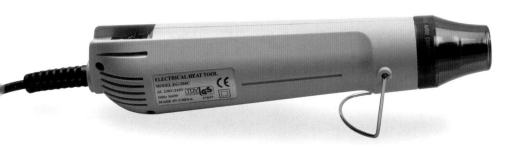

A heat gun is needed for embossing, which is probably the most popular way of decorating a stamp. Heat guns are also useful for drying stamped images quickly so you can continue working on a project.
Embossing liquid comes in various forms; a pen, as shown, and an ink pad are the most useful.

Embossing powders come in many colors and finishes. Always pour any excess powder back into the jar to be used again.

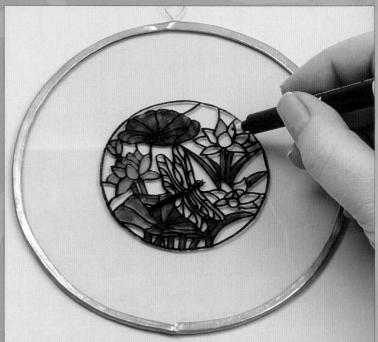

THE TECHNIQUES

When you start a new craft, there are always some basic techniques to master. As you gain in confidence and your skills grow, you will want to explore further and try more creative techniques that test your abilities and allow you to express your ideas more fully. This book will act as a guide to those of you who are just starting out in stamping and will be an inspiration and tutor as

your skills develop. Even if you are a seasoned stamper, you will still find much of interest. There are many exciting techniques—some of which have been developed especially for this book— for coloring, decorating, and using stamps to their fullest. There are also new twists on traditional techniques to try, plus lots of helpful hints and professional tips.

MAKING A STAMP

There are hundreds of ready-made stamps available, but sometimes you just can't find exactly what you need. So for that personalized card or to match an existing pattern or fit a particular area, make your own stamp. This chapter looks at different stamp materials and the kinds of motifs to use with them. These motifs are shown on a small scale; to find them on a larger scale or more of them, turn to the Motif library (see page 138).

TRANSFERRING A MOTIF

You can use the traditional tracing method to transfer a motif onto stamping media (see panel below right), or you can use carbon paper. Carbon paper works best on firm, matte media and offers a quick and easy way of transferring a motif from which to make your own stamp.

1 Lay the carbon paper, carbon-side down, on top of the stamping media, in this case a piece of wet-and-grow sponge. Lay the motif you want to transfer on top of the carbon paper (see *Motif library*, page 138).

2 Draw over the lines of the motif with a pencil. Press firmly to ensure that all the lines are transferred onto the sponge.

3 Remove the motif and carbon paper to reveal the transferred design.

Motifs of any sort can be transferred onto most stamping media using carbon paper. If you want to transfer onto fabric, there is a special dressmaker's carbon paper available.

TRACING METHOD

If you don't have carbon paper, then trace the motif onto ordinary tracing paper. Using a soft pencil, scribble over the back of the traced lines. Lay the tracing paper in position on the material you want to use, scribbled side down. Draw firmly over the traced lines again to transfer the image.

HIGH-DENSITY FOAM STAMP

High-density foam is available in craft stores and is easily cut and shaped with a knife. Since it is thick, it is easy to hold and doesn't need to be mounted onto a backboard.

1 Using a permanent pen, draw the shape you want to stamp onto the foam. Cut out the basic outline with a sharp knife. Be very careful when using a knife, and never cut toward your hand.

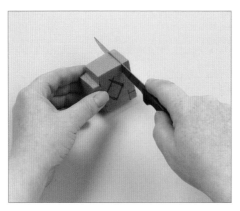

2 Carefully cut out the shaping around the edge of the stamp.

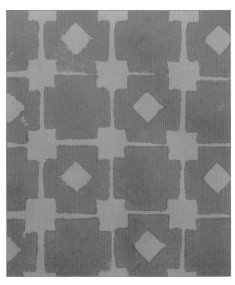

Bold shapes work well when used to stamp an all-over pattern.

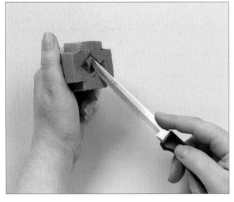

3 Cut around the edge of the internal shape, ensuring that you don't cut right through the foam. Use the tip of the knife to carefully cut away the foam inside the internal shape.

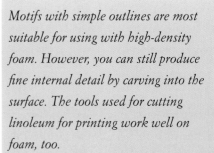

4 Ink up the stamp (see *Choosing the right medium*, page 33) and press it down onto the surface you want to stamp (see *Stamping on different surfaces*, pages 38–45). Lift it off cleanly to reveal the stamped design.

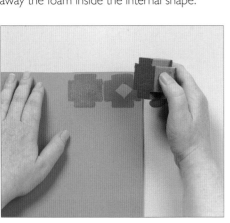

5 Turn the stamp over and repeat the process. The other side of the foam stamp will produce the same shape, but without the internal detail.

Motifs with simple outlines are most suitable for using with high-density foam. However, you can still produce fine internal detail by carving into the surface. The tools used for cutting linoleum for printing work well on foam, too.

STRING STAMP

Outline stamps can easily be made with string, though fine household string can be difficult to ink up cleanly. Make your stamp with thick string or cord, such as the piping cord used here.

1 Spread some craft adhesive on a block of MDF (medium-density fiberboard) in roughly the shape of the stamp you want to make.

2 Press one end of the string down onto the middle of the glued area. Holding it down with one finger, coil the string around, pressing it down onto the adhesive as you go.

The texture of the string will also influence the stamp. Smooth string usually gives a better result than the hairy kind.

3 Continue coiling the string around, pressing it down as you work. Leave a narrow gap between the coils. When you reach the edge of the glue, cut the string and press the end down firmly. Leave the stamp to dry facedown.

4 Use an ink pad to color the string (see *Using ink pads*, page 33), and press it down onto the surface you want to stamp (see *Stamping on different surfaces*, pages 38–45). Lift it off cleanly to reveal the stamped design.

String is best used to make outline stamps with just one continuous line, as it can be tricky to cut short pieces and stick them down tidily in the right place. Experiment with different thicknesses of string to determine the best one to use with a particular motif.

SPONGE STAMP

You can make a stamp from most kinds of sponge; kitchen sponge and bath sponge both work well. Here we have used wet-and-grow sponge, which is thin and easy to cut out when it is dry. However, when it is soaked in water, it swells up and is an ideal medium for stamping with. Wet-and-grow sponge is available in all good craft stores.

The texture of the sponge will, of course, affect the stamped image, so do consider this when choosing a sponge to stamp with.

1 Transfer a motif onto the dry sponge (see *Transferring a motif*, page 13). Using sharp scissors, carefully cut it out.

2 Place the sponge in water and let it expand. Squeeze out any excess water and leave it to dry until it is only just damp.

3 Brush paint onto the sponge (see *Brushing a stamp*, page 34).

4 Position the sponge over the surface you want to stamp (see *Stamping on different surfaces*, pages 38–45). Pat the back of the sponge to ensure that all of it comes into contact with the surface.

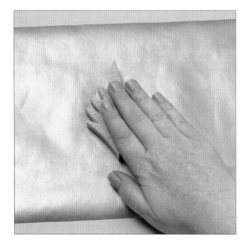

5 Lift the sponge cleanly off the surface to reveal the stamped design.

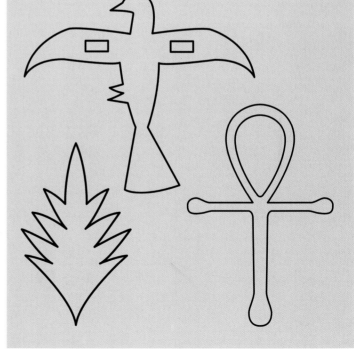

When choosing a motif to use with a sponge stamp, look for one with connected, solid areas. The motif can be quite detailed, but fine lines or intricate patterns are not suitable.

CORK STAMP

Cork tiles and coasters can be used to make simple stamps, and the textured surface can produce an interesting effect. This medium is not suitable for complex designs or fine lines, however, since cork tends to crumble while being cut.

1 Draw two concentric squares on a cork coaster. Using a craft knife and a steel rule, cut out both squares.

2 Decide which face of the cork you want to stamp with—one side is usually less textured than the other. Brush paint onto the cork (see *Brushing a stamp*, page 34).

A design stamped with household items—a coaster and a bottle work.

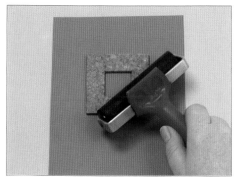

3 Press the cork down onto the surface you want to stamp (see *Stamping on different surfaces*, pages 38–45). Roll over it with a brayer to ensure that all of the cork comes into contact with the surface.

4 Lift the cork off cleanly to reveal the stamped design.

5 You can also use a bottle cork to stamp with. Choose one that has a fairly flat end. Brush paint onto one end of the cork.

6 Press the painted end down onto the paper and cleanly lift it off.

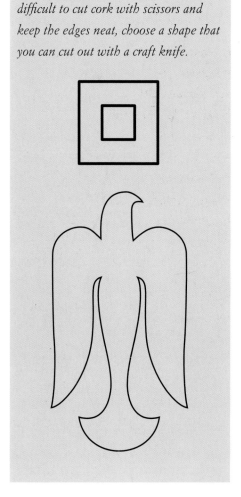

It is best to use simple, bold shapes when making cork stamps. Since it is difficult to cut cork with scissors and keep the edges neat, choose a shape that you can cut out with a craft knife.

RUBBER-SHEET STAMP

Self-adhesive rubber sheet is an ideal material to use to make stamps. You can cut complex shapes from it and stick them to a backboard of card, hardboard, or MDF (medium-density fiberboard). The rubber sheet is quite thin, so it is better to stick two pieces together to create a thicker stamp.

Rubber sheet is a good medium for making stamps with separate elements.

SEPARATE ELEMENTS

If the design you want to use has several separate elements, then transfer it onto the block of MDF, as well as onto the rubber. Then, when you cut out the rubber, you can simply stick the elements to the MDF in the correct positions, following the transferred lines.

1 Cut two pieces of self-adhesive rubber sheet to the same size. Peel the paper backing off one piece.

2 Stick the first piece to the rubber surface of the second piece.

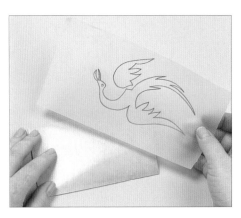

3 Transfer a motif (see *Motif library*, page 138) onto the paper backing of the second piece. As the surface is shiny, it may be best to use the tracing method (see *Transferring a Motif*, page 13).

4 Draw firmly over the traced lines to transfer the motif onto the backing paper. If necessary, tape the motif in place to ensure that it does not slip.

5 Using sharp scissors, carefully cut out the motif.

6 Peel off the paper backing and stick the rubber elements to a block of MDF.

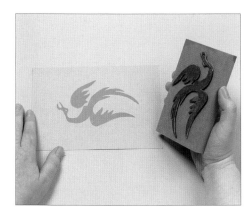

7 Ink up the stamp (see *Choosing the right medium*, page 33) and press it down onto the surface you want to stamp (see *Stamping on different surfaces*, pages 38–45). Lift it off cleanly to reveal the stamped design.

Since rubber sheet can be cut to produce fine lines and separate elements, most motifs are suitable to be used with it. However, if the motif is very complex, you may find it easier to cut it out of a single thickness of rubber, but be sure to take care when inking it up.

GLASS OUTLINER STAMP

If your craft interests include glass painting, then make use of this in your stamping projects, too. Glass painting outliner can be used to make very detailed stamps, as detailed as your skill with the outliner allows. The stamp will be quite shallow, so it is best to use a fairly dry inking technique; an ink pad is ideal.

On thick plastic film

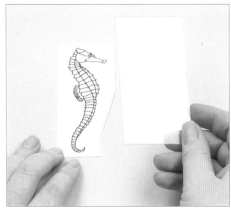

I Lay a motif (see *Motif library*, page 138) underneath a piece of thick plastic film.

2 Fill an outlining bag with glass painting outliner, or, if you prefer, use the outliner straight from the tube. Outline the design onto the plastic, following the lines of the motif underneath. Leave the outliner to dry.

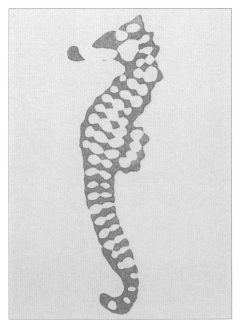

Mounting the outlined motif on rubber sheet allows it to "give" a little and will produce a clearer stamp.

3 Cut a piece of self-adhesive rubber sheet large enough to cover the motif, and peel off the paper backing.

4 Stick the rubber onto the back of the plastic, ensuring that it covers the whole of the motif.

Glass painting outliner can be used to make very intricate outline shapes, but it is not suitable for making solid, filled-in shapes, since the surface will not be flat. If you have never used outliner before, start by making simple stamps, and progress to more complex ones as your skills improve.

5 Cut a piece of double-sided sticky film the same size as the rubber sheet. Peel off the paper backing on one side and stick it to the back of the rubber.

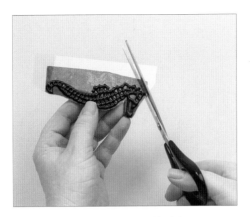

6 Cut out the outlined motif with household scissors, cutting through all the layers at the same time. Cut as close as possible to the outliner.

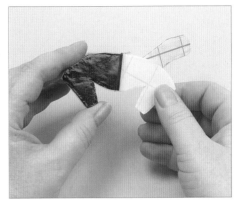

7 Peel the remaining paper backing off the double-sided film.

8 Stick the rubber onto a block of MDF. You can substitute cardboard or hardboard for MDF, but the thicker the backing is, the easier the stamp is to hold and use.

9 Use an ink pad (see *Using ink pads*, page 33) to ink up the stamp and press it down onto the surface you want to stamp (see *Stamping on different surfaces*, pages 38–45). Lift it off cleanly to reveal the stamped design.

OUTLINING ONTO RELEASE PAPER OR THIN FILM

You can also outline a design onto release paper (below right). Once the outliner has dried, peel it off the paper, spray-glue onto the back of it, and stick it onto a piece of rubber, which in turn can be stuck onto a block of MDF.

Alternatively, you can outline the design onto thin plastic film (left), cut it out, and stick it onto rubber and a block of MDF.

You can also outline a stamp directly onto a piece of self-adhesive rubber sheet. This produces a stamp with more "give," which is better if the surface you want to stamp is textured.

On rubber

1 Lay a piece of white-transfer carbon paper on top of a piece of self-adhesive rubber sheet, carbon-side down. Lay a motif (see *Motif library*, page 138) on top of the carbon paper.

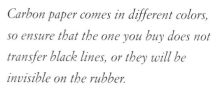

Carbon paper comes in different colors, so ensure that the one you buy does not transfer black lines, or they will be invisible on the rubber.

2 Use pieces of masking tape to stick the motif and carbon paper to the rubber sheet. Draw over the lines to transfer the motif onto the rubber (see *Transferring a motif*, page 13).

3 Outline the design onto the rubber sheet, following the transferred lines. Leave the outliner to dry.

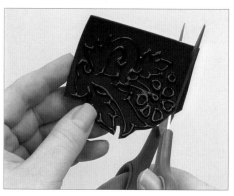

4 Cut out the design with household scissors, cutting as close as possible to the outliner.

5 Peel the paper backing off the self-adhesive rubber sheet.

6 Stick the rubber onto a block of MDF.

7 Use an ink pad (see *Using ink pads*, page 33) to ink up the stamp and press it down onto the surface you want to stamp (see *Stamping on different surfaces*, pages 38–45). Lift it off cleanly to reveal the stamped design.

POTATO STAMP

Many of us made stamps from potatoes when we were in school, but these were usually rather messy. Using a cookie cutter means that the lines and shapes are much cleaner, producing a more attractive stamp.

The shapes you can cut are dictated by the cookie cutters you can find, but cutters come in a variety of shapes, so look for the most interesting ones.

1 Cut a large potato in half. Press a cookie cutter down into the cut face. Press the cutter about ½ inch (1 cm) into the face.

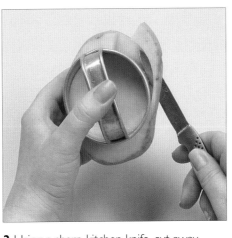

2 Using a sharp kitchen knife, cut away about ½ inch (1 cm) of the excess potato. Cut right up to the edge of the cookie cutter. Gently pull the cutter off the potato. Be careful when using a knife, and never cut toward your hand.

3 Press a smaller cookie cutter into the cutout shape.

4 Remove the cutter and carefully cut out the potato from within it. Leave the potato facedown on some kitchen paper for a few minutes to absorb any excess moisture.

5 Ink up the potato stamp (see *Choosing the right medium*, page 33) and press it down onto the surface you want to stamp (see *Stamping on different surfaces*, pages 38–45). Lift it off cleanly to reveal the stamped design.

PUNCHED STAMP

With a hobby punch

This is one of the easiest stamps you can make yourself. It doesn't require any artistic skill, just rubber sheet and a shaped punch.

Arrange punched-out shapes in patterns to make rather complex stamps.

single stamp

I Punch a shape, as before, and stick it onto a plastic bottle top. This makes an easy-to-use, instant backing for a stamp.

I Use a hobby punch to punch shapes out of a strip of self-adhesive rubber sheet.

2 Peel the backing paper off each punched shape in turn.

2 Ink up the stamp (see *Choosing the right medium*, page 33) and press it down onto the surface you want to stamp (see *Stamping on different surfaces*, pages 38–45). Lift it off cleanly to reveal the stamped design.

---

3 Stick the shapes onto a store-bought stamp backing or onto a block of MDF.

4 Ink up the stamp (see *Choosing the right medium*, page 33) and press it down onto the surface you want to stamp (see *Stamping on different surfaces*, pages 38–45). Lift it off cleanly to reveal the stamped design.

PUNCHING STAMPS

Hobby punches are widely available in an enormous range of shapes and sizes. They provide an excellent way of making quick, easy, no-mess stamps.

With a die-cutter

Hobby die-cutters are becoming increasingly popular and can be used in many crafts. They provide a great way of making larger stamps, with all the ease of a hobby punch.

Dies are available in a wide range of designs, most of which are perfect for making stamps.

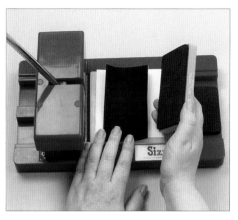

1 Lay a piece of self-adhesive rubber sheet on the base of the die-cutter. Lay the die you want to use on top of the rubber.

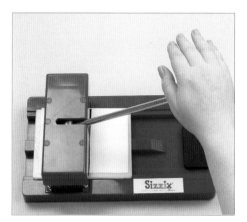

2 Slide the rubber and die into the machine, and press down on the handle. Different machines work in different ways, so make sure that you follow all of the manufacturer's instructions.

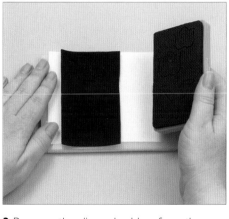

3 Remove the die and rubber from the machine. Gently lift the die off the rubber.

4 Carefully peel away the excess rubber to reveal the cutout shapes.

5 Peel the paper backing off the shapes and stick them onto a block of MDF.

6 Ink up the stamp (see *Choosing the right medium*, page 33) and press it down onto the surface you want to stamp (see *Stamping on different surfaces*, pages 38–45). Lift it off cleanly to reveal the stamped design.

BORDER STAMP

Framing a stamped design with a border can unite the various elements and finish off the project perfectly. This technique allows you to make a border stamp to complement a main stamp, especially if you have also made the main stamp.

If you find it difficult to hold the thin piece of plastic, you can glue a piece of MDF to the center back to act as a handle.

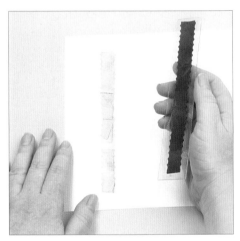

1 Using decorative scissors, cut a strip of self-adhesive rubber sheet. When cutting, close the blades of the scissors fully on the rubber, then open them out again and carefully realign the pattern before continuing to cut. This will ensure that the decorative edge is consistent all the way along. Trim both ends of the rubber at matching points in the pattern.

2 Peel the paper backing off the rubber and stick it to a piece of clear, thick plastic. Using a clear backing allows you to realign the stamp perfectly when stamping a long border.

3 Ink up the stamp (see *Choosing the right medium*, page 33) and press it down onto the surface you want to stamp (see *Stamping on different surfaces*, pages 38–45). Lift it off cleanly to reveal the stamped design.

USING DECORATIVE SCISSORS

Decorative scissors are available in a wide range of patterns (left). As well as cutting border stamps, they provide a good way of making edges for solid stamps (below right). Here they have been used to edge a punched-heart stamp (see *Punched stamp*, page 24). You can also make a stamp by cutting several strips of rubber using different-edged scissors (far right). Stick all the strips to one block of MDF and use it to shadow-stamp backgrounds (see *Shadow stamping*, page 83).

NEGATIVE STAMP

This technique allows you to make a negative image from a positive rubber stamp. This technique works best with fairly simple, graphic designs.

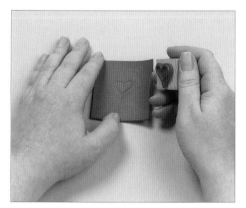

1 Use a heat gun to warm a piece of soft, foam-rubber sheet. When the edges of the sheet start to curl, it is warm enough.

You can make an effective design by using the negative stamp, and the stamp it was made from, together.

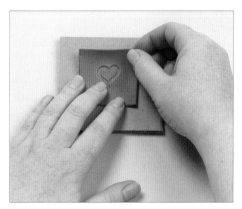

2 Press the stamp into the foam before it cools. Press hard and hold the stamp in position for about a minute. Lift the stamp off to reveal the negative imprint.

3 Stick two pieces of thick cardboard together with all-purpose adhesive to make a backboard. Stick the foam to the cardboard, again using all-purpose adhesive.

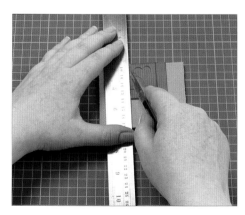

4 Using a craft knife and steel rule, cut the foam and card to the size you want. Cut through all the layers together.

5 Ink up the stamp (see *Choosing the right medium*, page 33) and press it down onto the surface you want to stamp (see *Stamping on different surfaces*, pages 38–45). Lift it off cleanly to reveal the stamped design.

6 Ink up the positive stamp you made your stamp from and stamp next to the negative design to make a pattern.

CHOOSING A STAMP

There are thousands of stamps available in craft stores and hobby centers, making it difficult to select just the right one for a particular project. Stamps can also be expensive, so you want to be sure that you are getting the right one, or you could be wasting your money. This chapter looks at the different types of stamps available and the best uses for each.

RUBBER STAMPS

Despite the name, these stamps are very seldom made from rubber these days. Modern plastics have taken over, though the stamp faces are often still colored the classic red of rubber. There are a number of different types of these stamps.

The working face of the stamp is called the "die." Generally speaking, the deeper the etched design, the better the quality of the stamp. A deep etch also makes the stamp easier to use, since you are less likely to get unwanted ink smears from the stamp background on your project. Another sign of a good-quality stamp is that the die is trimmed closely around the edges of the etched design; this also lessens the chances of unwanted smudges. It is possible to trim away any excess rubber with a craft knife if the stamp does smudge. Rubber stamp designs range from single motifs (right), to solid-shape designs (below left), to complex all-over designs (below right).

Art stamps are very fine-line stamps that produce beautiful images. They are usually of the highest quality, with hardwood backs, and are expensive. Look after them well, cleaning them carefully every time you use them (see *Cleaning a stamp*, page 37). If you want to emboss an art stamp, you will need to use an extra-fine embossing powder to pick up all the detail clearly.

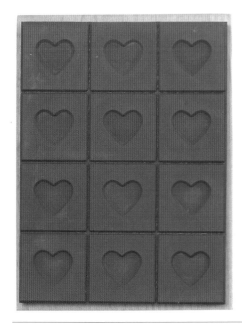

Letter stamp sets are a very useful thing to have in your stamp collection. They are available in various typefaces, but because they are quite expensive, it is a good idea to choose a set that is quite plain so that it will be suitable for most projects. Use the technique for *Stamping in a straight line* (see page 48) to place them accurately.

FOAM STAMPS

Foam stamps generally have simpler, solid motifs and are much less expensive than rubber stamps. They are good to use with children, since they are easy to handle, and it doesn't matter as much if they get spoiled. There are two types of foam stamps—hard stamps and soft stamps.

Hard foam stamps will produce good, clear designs as long as you do not over-ink them. There is nowhere for any excess ink to go—other than onto the surface you are stamping on—so if you apply too much ink, it will just smudge out around the edges of the stamp and blur the image. If you want to apply ink to a foam stamp, it is best to use a roller (see *Rollering a stamp*, page 35). They also work well with paint (see *Brushing a stamp*, page 34).

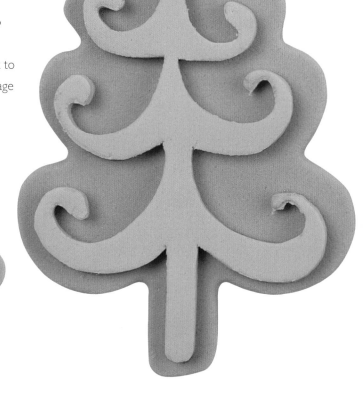

Soft foam stamps absorb a lot of color, so they are best used with paints (see *Choosing the right medium*, page 33). You can brush the paint onto the stamp (see *Brushing a stamp*, page 34), or you can dip it into the paint. To do this, spread some paint out quite thinly on a plate. Dab the surface of the stamp onto it, making sure that all of it is covered. Soft foam stamps are usually lightly textured, and this texture will show on the stamped image.

STAMP BACKINGS

The backing of a stamp is sometimes called the "mount." Most stamps have a wooden backing that is either a block of wood or has an integral handle, making them easier to use. The best stamps have a hardwood backing, which is long-lasting and should give you years of use. Plastic-backed stamps are generally less expensive, and acrylic-backed stamps are becoming more popular.

Large wooden-backed stamps often have a gently curved stamping surface (top right). This allows you to roll the stamp onto the surface you are working on, making it easier to ensure that the whole die comes into contact with the working surface. Smaller stamps are usually flat (below right), as there is less chance of poor contact, or of wrinkling the working surface when stamping a small image.

Inexpensive stamps, especially foam ones, often have a molded plastic back (below). They are easy to hold but are much lighter than wooden-backed stamps, so you need to apply more pressure to get a crisp image.

Clear acrylic stamps are becoming more popular, since they are so easy to use. Though the backing plate is often shallow, you can see exactly where you are putting the stamp, making it easier to position them accurately.

The stamp shown here (right) also has the advantage of a removable die. You can just peel it off and wash it with water to clean it. The back of the die is tacky, so as soon as it is dry, it will cling to the acrylic backing plate again. You need only a few backing plates, and the flat stamps are easy to catalogue and store. They are also relatively inexpensive.

The clear design can be hard to see, so stamp onto scrap paper using a permanent black ink pad. This will stain the die a little, making it easier to see the design. The tacky surface also tends to attract fluff and dust, so work in a clean area.

Roller stamps come in various sizes, from mini to jumbo. Some contain ink cartridges and are therefore self-inking. If the cartridge is removable, then you can change the ink color as often as you wish. You can even buy cartridges of embossing ink.

Other roller stamps need to be inked up by wheeling them over an ink pad. If you are careful, you can ink up different sections of the wheel with different colors and produce a multicolored image.

INKING A STAMP

The medium you choose to apply to a stamp depends on the surface on which you will be stamping (see *Stamping on different surfaces*, pages 38–45). The way in which you apply the medium to the stamp depends on the medium itself. This chapter offers advice on choosing a medium and then shows you the various different methods of getting the color onto a stamp so that you can start to work.

CHOOSING THE RIGHT MEDIUM

You can stamp an image onto almost any surface, as long as you use the right medium. There are various specialist inks and paints available for stamping onto surfaces such as ceramics and fabrics, and these are covered in the appropriate chapters in this book. However, most stamping is done on paper or card, and the best media to use are ink pads, brush pens, or paints.

Ink pads

Ink pads are specially designed for stamping with and are therefore the most popular medium, especially if you are using fine-line stamps. There are two basic types: dye-based inks, which have a felt pad, and pigment inks, which have a foam pad. Dye-based inks dry faster than pigment inks, though the drying time will depend on the paper you are stamping. Some dye-based inks are waterproof when dry, which is useful if you want to watercolor the design (see *Coloring a stamp*, page 52–57). Pigment inks take longer to dry and are therefore suitable for embossing. Be aware that unless they are embossed, some pigment inks never dry completely and will leave a waxy residue on the paper, which will smudge if touched. Unless they are embossed, pigment inks are not waterproof (see also *Using ink pads*, page 33).

Brush pens

Brush pens work well on fine stamps, though you have to coat the stamp quickly or the ink will dry. They can be used to color a stamp in one shade or to apply several colors to a single stamp (see also *Using brush pens*, page 34).

Paint

You can use any water-based paint to stamp with, though the final image from a rubber stamp will never be as crisp as one made with an ink pad. It is better to use paint with a large foam stamp, unless you want a rougher look. Don't use solvent or oil-based paints, as they can ruin the stamp, and if you use acrylic paint, clean the stamp immediately after use. Watercolor paint will dry up quite quickly, so it is not suitable for a large stamp. Use watercolor paint from a tube, not from a palette (see also *Brushing a stamp*, page 34).

USING INK PADS

Ink pads are available in an enormous range of colors and finishes, including metallics, rainbow stripes, and embossing medium in different colors. Most ink pads have lids that can be either folded right back or removed completely to make inking easier.

Using an ink pad will make it easier to produce a sharp, clean stamped image.

1 Unless the stamp is very large, take the ink pad to the stamp rather than the other way around. This makes it easier to ensure that you do not over-ink the stamp, and it will be easier to see that it is fully inked. Pat the pad onto the surface of the stamp; do not wipe over it since you will wipe the ink off again.

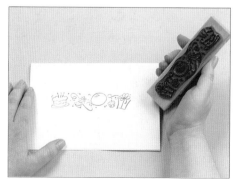

2 Press the stamp down onto the surface you want to stamp (see *Stamping on different surfaces*, pages 38–45). Lift it off cleanly to reveal the stamped design.

USING BRUSH PENS

Brush pens are most useful when you want to apply different colors to different areas of a stamp and can be blended on the stamp to produce further shades.

Sensitive use of colored brush pens can make a single stamped image much more interesting.

I Draw over the raised lines of the die with the brush pen. You need to work quite quickly, as the ink will not stay wet for very long, though you can refresh it by breathing on it before you stamp.

2 Press the stamp down onto the surface you want to stamp (see *Stamping on different surfaces*, pages 38–45). Lift it off cleanly to reveal the stamped design.

BRUSHING A STAMP

Water-based paints can be used to ink up a stamp, though if you use acrylic paint, you must clean the stamp immediately after using it, or it will be ruined.

Paint will not produce as crisp an outline as an ink pad or even a brush pen.

I Squeeze some paint out of the tube onto a plate. Use a fine, soft paintbrush to brush the paint onto the stamp die.

2 Press the stamp down onto the surface you want to stamp (see *Stamping on different surfaces*, pages 38–45). Lift it off cleanly to reveal the stamped design.

ROLLERING A STAMP

A brayer is a special hard roller designed for inking up a stamp. You can buy large ink pads, wide enough to accommodate a brayer, or you can just move the brayer along a small pad, inking one part of it at a time.

1 Roll the brayer in one direction across the ink pad, ensuring that it is evenly covered in ink.

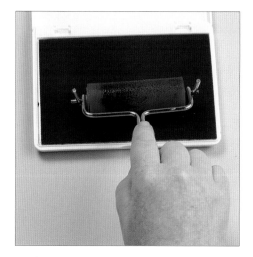

2 Roll the brayer across the face of the stamp. Again roll in one direction, not backward and forward.

3 Press the stamp down onto the surface you want to stamp (see *Stamping on different surfaces*, pages 38–45). Lift it off cleanly to reveal the stamped design.

A brayer is particularly useful if you are inking a large stamp with dye-based ink, since the ink will start to dry as soon as it touches the stamp. The brayer allows you to cover the whole stamp in ink very quickly.

> **ROLLERING ON A RAINBOW PAD**
> If you are inking up from a rainbow pad, roll the brayer over it in the direction of the stripes to avoid mixing the colors together.

MAKING A PAINT PAD

This is a particularly useful technique when you want to use a specific shade of ink or paint that you cannot find in a store-bought ink pad. It also works well if you are stamping with food coloring (see *Using food coloring*, page 87) or masking fluid (see *Stamping with masking fluid*, page 65).

1 Cut a piece of kitchen foil approximately 12 inches (30 cm) square. Fold the foil in half and then fold over a narrow strip on each edge. This will help to keep the foil flat.

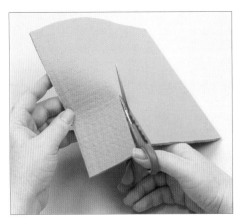

2 Cut a piece of kitchen sponge approximately 3 inches (8 cm) square.

3 Place the sponge on the foil, positioning it toward one end.

4 Drip a little ink (or whatever stamping medium you want to use) onto the center of the sponge. If necessary, brush the ink out across the sponge with a paintbrush.

5 Press the stamp onto the ink pad in the usual way (see *Using ink pads*, page 33).

6 Press the stamp onto the surface you want to work on (see *Stamping on different surfaces*, pages 38–45).

7 When you have finished using the stamp, fold the foil over it and fold in all the edges to seal it. This will stop the ink evaporating so that you can use the pad again. If you want to keep it for a length of time, place the sealed pad in a plastic bag to keep it as damp as possible.

CLEANING A STAMP

The method you choose to clean a stamp that will depend on how dirty it is. If the stamp has been kept in good condition and only just been used, then a baby wipe will suffice. Any dirtier than that, it's best to use a specialist stamp cleaner. A stamp with congealed paint on the face is best cleaned on a mat, and if that fails, then you will have to use a toothbrush. Do not be tempted to wash a stamp under the tap or to submerge it in water. The water will break down the glue that holds the stamp to the backing material.

With baby wipes

Simply wipe the ink off the stamp with an alcohol- and lanolin-free baby wipe. It is important that the wipe is alcohol-free, or over time repeated cleaning will damage the rubber surface. Lanolin will leave a residue on the surface, and next time you use the stamp, ink will not stick to it properly. Some solvent-based inks do stain the die, but as long as the wipe comes away from the die clean, this does not matter.

With stamp cleaner

1 There are many specialist stamp cleaners on the market for removing dried ink from a stamp. Rub the cleaner over the rubber, pushing it into the nooks and crannies as much as possible.

2 Wipe off the cleaning solution with a baby wipe, as before. If you are using the stamp again immediately, dry it with a tissue to remove all traces of the cleaning fluid.

With a mat

If the stamp is very dirty, spread a specialist cleaner over the die, then scrub the stamp back and forth on a cleaning mat. These mats can be bought in craft stores, but you can use a piece of stiff-pile carpet instead. Use a baby wipe, as before, to wipe the surface clean. No matter how well you usually clean them, most stamps will benefit from a periodic scrub.

With a toothbrush

If the stamp has a lot of dried ink on it, then a toothbrush is the best tool for cleaning it. Spread a specialist cleaner over the rubber, then scrub it with the toothbrush, forcing the bristles right into the surface detail. Use a baby wipe, as before, to wipe the surface clean.

STAMPING ON DIFFERENT SURFACES

Almost any reasonably smooth surface is of interest to the enthusiastic stamper, from conventional surfaces—such as paper and walls—to materials such as sandpaper and CDs. This chapter illustrates the techniques for stamping on all of the most popular surfaces, plus a few unusual ones to whet your appetite!

PAPER AND CARD

The most commonly used materials to stamp on are paper and card. However, there are different types of both, and the techniques for stamping onto them vary a little.

On smooth paper

Ink up the stamp (see *Choosing the right medium*, page 33) and press it down onto the paper. Press firmly, being careful not to move the stamp at all or the design will be blurred. Lift the stamp cleanly straight up off the card to reveal the stamped design.

On card

Stamping onto smooth card uses the same technique as stamping onto smooth paper. These are the ideal materials for the beginner stamper to work on. As you become more confident, try stamping onto textured paper and other materials.

On textured paper

Stamping onto textured paper or card requires a little more ink on the surface of the stamp and a little more pressure, as you have to push the ink into the texture. The heavier the texture, the more ink and pressure needed. Very textured surfaces, such as corrugated card, cannot be stamped onto successfully.

On vellum

Stamping onto vellum requires a special ink—available in craft stores—as ordinary inks will tend to bleed on the porous surface. Do not press too hard on the stamp or it may slip, smudging the design.

MOUNTING A STAMP

An image can be stamped onto a smooth paper or card for ease of stamping, then cut out and mounted onto a textured background for a more interesting-looking finish. Depending on the degree of texture to which you are sticking the paper, use either double-sided tape or adhesive to stick it down. If the surface is lightly textured, then tape will work well. Paper adhesive or spray glue can be used on a medium-textured surface, and for a heavily textured surface, use craft adhesive. Be aware that adhesive can mark thin paper, so stamp onto fairly thick smooth paper.

If you are mounting a vellum stamp onto another piece of paper, you need to be careful that the glue does not show. Paper adhesive and tape will show through the translucent surface, though some tapes show less than others. Spray glue or a machine that applies glue to the back of paper are the best products to use. Alternatively, you can place further decoration on the front of the stamp to hide any tape or glue marks.

WALLS

Stamping is a great way to add personal, decorative elements to a room scheme. Stamping on a large scale does take some time, so prepare everything in advance, and leave enough time to complete the job without rushing.

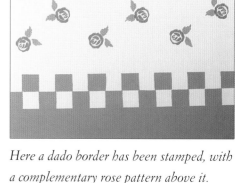

1 Paint the top half of the wall in a rich cream color, and the bottom half, below dado height, in a soft green. Measure the height you want the first line of checks to be—here it was 3 inches (7 cm)—and make pencil marks at this height across the wall. Make a mark approximately every 12 inches (30 cm).

Here a dado border has been stamped, with a complementary rose pattern above it. However, you can stamp almost any design, so choose a pattern to complement existing furnishings or color schemes.

2 Stick a length of low-tack tape right across the wall, just above the pencil marks.

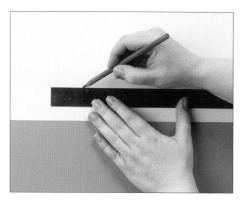

3 Make a pencil mark every 3 inches (7 cm) along the tape.

4 Cut a sponge to 3 inches (7 cm) square. Dip the sponge into the same green paint you used on the wall, and stamp a row of alternate squares between the tape and the green-painted part of the wall. Use the marks on the masking tape to guide you in positioning the stamp.

5 Peel off the tape and leave the paint to dry completely.

6 Stick a length of tape across the wall, aligning it with the tops of the stamped squares. Stick another length 3 inches (7 cm) above the first length.

7 Stamp another row of squares, ensuring that you alternate them with the first row to produce a checkerboard pattern.

8 Peel off both lengths of tape and leave the paint to dry.

9 Brush dusky pink paint onto the petals of a large rose stamp, and the soft green paint onto the leaves (see *Brushing a stamp*, page 34).

10 Stamp a pattern of roses above the dado rail. Repaint the stamp every time you use it to keep the color levels even.

WOOD

You can stamp onto wood with a variety of media, but stamp pads are the quickest and easiest to use. Ensure that the wood is flat, or the stamp will not reproduce properly.

You can stamp onto plain wood, or you can undercoat it with emulsion paint.

I Use an ink pad to color the stamp (see *Using ink pads*, page 33).

2 Press the stamp carefully down onto the wood, pressing firmly to ensure that all of the ink is transferred. Lift the stamp off carefully. Leave to dry, then seal the wood with matte varnish.

STAMPING ON FURNITURE

You can use this technique to stamp designs onto items of furniture. Remember that it is difficult to stamp onto curved surfaces with a large stamp, so choose smaller stamps to decorate things such as the legs of tables or spindle backs of chairs.

GLASS

Stamping offers a quick and easy way of transferring an outline onto glass. The outline can be colored in or left as it is.

With ink

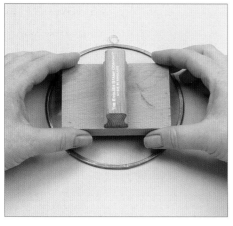

2 Press the stamp onto the glass. Do not press too firmly or you risk cracking the glass.

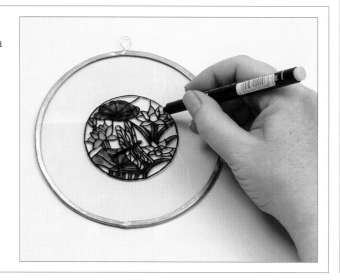

Stamping works best on flat glass, though with care you can stamp onto shallow curves.

I Ink up the stamp using a permanent ink pad (see *Using ink pads*, page 33).

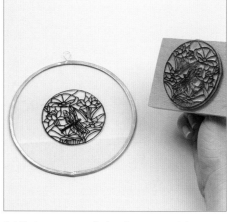

3 Lift the stamp off cleanly to reveal the stamped design.

COLORING A DESIGN
The easiest way to color a stamped design is with felt-tipped pens. Use the translucent type that are usually sold for marking acetate for an overhead projector. Allow one color to dry before coloring an adjacent area with a different color.

Using overhead projector pens, you can stamp in different colors straight onto glass. Choose permanent pens rather than water-based ones, or the project may smudge if it gets wet.

Use the same stamp with different colors each time, or color sections of the stamp in different shades and stamp a multicolored image.

With pens

I Use overhead projector pens to apply color straight onto the stamp die (see *Using brush pens*, page 34).

2 Press the stamp down onto the glass and lift it off cleanly to reveal the design.

STAMPING USING PENS
You need to work quite fast with this technique, or the ink from the pens will dry before you have time to stamp. Clean the stamp immediately after use.

GLAZED TILES

You can decorate plain tiles with stamps and permanent or specialist inks. There are various kinds of inks available, but do follow the manufacturer's instructions for the best results.

You can decorate tiles with an all-over pattern, as shown, or with a single centerpiece (see Stamping an abstract pattern, *page 50, and* Positioning a centerpiece, *page 51).*

I Ink up the stamp with a permanent or a special ceramic ink pad (see *Using ink pads*, page 33).

2 Press the stamp onto the tile. Do not press too hard or the stamp may slip on the glazed surface. Lift it off cleanly to reveal the design. The ink will take longer to dry than usual, so be careful not to smudge the stamps while you are working.

LOOKING AFTER TILES

Once the ink is dry, it is best to seal the stamped design with a coat of vanish. Clean the tiles by wiping them with a damp cloth; never scrub them.

CERAMICS

Stamps can also be used to decorate plates, bowls, and mugs. However, these should be used for decorative purposes only, not for serving food.

Plain, light-colored china is best for stamping onto, as the designs will show up well.

I Align the edge of the stamp with the base of the mug. Press one end of the stamp gently against the mug.

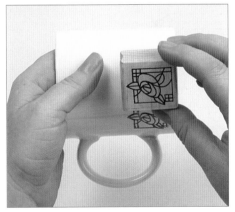

2 Holding the stamp still, turn the mug smoothly so that a section of it comes into contact with the stamp die. Keep turning the mug until it has rolled past the whole stamp.

STAMPING ON CURVES

The combination of shape and smooth surface means that it can be tricky to stamp onto curved ceramics. Practice the method shown above for the best results. Clean decorated items with a damp cloth and never scrub them or put them into a dishwasher.

SANDPAPER

You can stamp onto a huge variety of surfaces to create different effects. Fine-grit sandpaper works well; however, since the surface is rough, the stamped outline will not be completely solid. This slightly distressed effect can work well if you choose an appropriate design. Sandpaper can also look like stone, so stamps with ancient motifs work well, too.

Embellish the stamp with craft sand to add color and more texture.

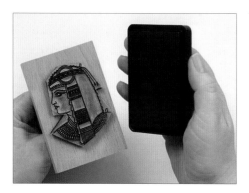

1 Use an archival, permanent ink pad to ink up the stamp (see *Using ink pads*, page 33).

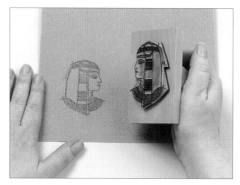

2 Press the stamp down onto the sandpaper, then lift it off cleanly to reveal the stamped design. Leave to dry.

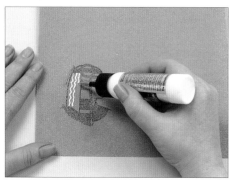

3 Pipe over some of the lines of the design with craft glue. Use a glue that comes in a bottle with a nozzle.

4 Put the sandpaper into a craft tray, or lay it on a piece of paper. Sprinkle fine, colored sand over the glued area.

5 Tip off the excess sand into the tray or onto the paper, and pour it back into the pot. Leave one colored area to dry before piping glue onto another area and sprinkling on a different-colored sand.

CDs

CDs are often given away free with magazines, and though you may not want the information on them, they do have other uses. For example, stamp and paint them and use them as coasters in the office or at home, or stick one to the front of a greeting card for a computer or music enthusiast. Once a CD has been stamped, don't put it in a computer or CD player.

Stamp several CDs with the same pattern to make a set of matching coasters.

1 Ink up the stamp with an archival ink pad and press it down onto the CD. Lift it off cleanly to reveal the stamped design. Leave to dry.

2 Lay the CD on a piece of scrap paper (shiny paper works best), and drip some acrylic paint onto the surface.

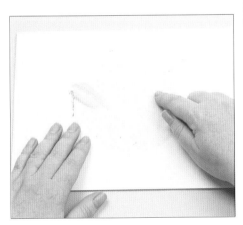

3 Place another piece of the same paper over the CD. Rub over the paper with your finger to smudge the paint across the CD. Do not rub for too long, or the colors will blend together too much.

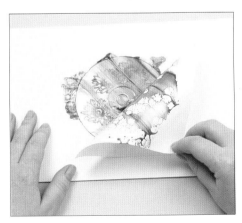

4 Peel off the top sheet of paper to reveal a multicolored, marbled pattern. Leave the CD to dry completely.

SHRINK PLASTIC

This is a fun medium to stamp onto, and the results can be used to make items such as key chains, refrigerator magnets, and jewelry.

1 Ink up the stamp (see *Choosing the right medium*, page 33) and press it down onto the surface you want to stamp (see *Stamping on different surfaces*, pages 38–45). Lift it off cleanly to reveal the stamped design. Color in the stamp with pencils.

2 Using sharp scissors, carefully cut out the stamped design.

3 Read the instructions on the packet of shrink plastic, and following them carefully, use a heat gun to shrink the plastic.

Fairly simple, easily recognizable designs work best with this technique. Complex images can be difficult to work out once the stamp has been shrunk.

SHRINKING PLASTIC

The pictures below show how much the plastic shrinks. The top picture shows the plastic before it was shrunk, next to an ink pad. The bottom picture shows the plastic after it was shrunk, next to the same ink pad.

4 If necessary, use something flat—the lid of a small ink pad is ideal—to flatten the plastic completely once it has shrunk. You must do this while the plastic is still soft.

POSITIONING A STAMP

Whether it be one stamp or several, how to accurately and most effectively position stamps on a surface is something that many novice stampers worry about. Do you just plunge in and stamp at random and hope it looks okay, or do you spend ages carefully measuring? Since neither solution fits every situation, learn instead how to achieve the best results by following the simple techniques demonstrated in this chapter.

POSITIONING A SINGLE STAMP

This can, of course, be done by eye or by measuring with a ruler, but if you are not confident in your ability to position a stamp correctly, the best tool to use is a stamp positioner. Both wooden and clear plastic positioners are available, and the advantage of the plastic ones is that you can see the whole surface you are stamping onto.

1 Lay the flat piece of plastic tightly against the right-angled piece. Ink up the stamp (see *Choosing the right medium*, page 33) and press it down onto the flat plastic. Make sure that the corner of the stamp backing is pressed into the right-angled piece of plastic.

2 Lift the stamp off cleanly to reveal the stamped design.

MAKING A POSITIONER
You can make your own stamp positioner from a right-angled piece of thick cardstock and sheet of tracing paper. You will need a fresh piece of tracing paper for each stamped image.

The positioner allows you to decide exactly where you want a stamp to be.

3 Decide where you want the stamp to be, and lay the flat plastic in place so that the stamp on it is in exactly the right spot. Push the right-angled piece of plastic up to it, as in Step 1.

4 Remove the piece of flat plastic, keeping the right-angled piece in exactly the right spot. Ink up the stamp (see *Choosing the right medium*, page 33) and press it down onto the paper, tight against the right angle.

5 Lift the stamp off cleanly to reveal the stamped design. Remove the right angle and use a baby wipe to clean the stamped design off the flat piece of plastic.

STAMPING IN A STRAIGHT LINE

This is a technique that many people find daunting, but by using a scrap piece of card with one straight edge and following the directions below, you'll be assured of success every time.

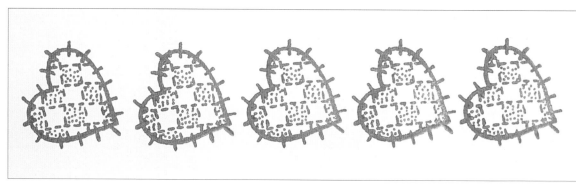

A perfectly straight line of hearts—simple!

1 Lay a straight edge of card across the surface you want to stamp (see *Stamping on different surfaces*, pages 38–45). If you want the line of stamps to be square to the edge, use a piece of card with two straight edges, and align one with the edge of the surface.

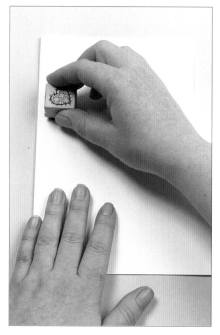

2 Ink up the stamp (see *Choosing the right medium*, page 33) and press it down onto the surface, aligning the square edge of the stamp backing with the straight edge of the card.

3 Lift the stamp off cleanly to reveal the stamped design.

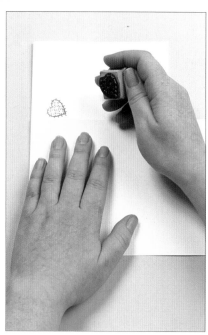

4 Continue in this way, aligning the edge of the stamp with the edge of the card each time you press it onto the surface.

STAMPING A REPEAT PATTERN

Stamping a regular pattern is another technique that, like stamping a straight line, people worry about. Again, it is actually easy to do; you just need to take your time and work methodically.

Odd numbers tend to look more pleasing to the eye than even ones.

1 Start stamping in one corner of the surface, aligning two edges of the stamp with the corner. Ink up the stamp (see *Choosing the right medium*, page 33) and press it down onto the surface (see *Stamping on different surfaces*, pages 38–45). Lift it off cleanly to reveal the stamped design.

2 Stamp the next image, aligning the corner of the stamp backing with a selected point on the first stamped image. This can be any point, as long as you use the same one throughout the project.

3 Continue in this way, always aligning the stamp with either the edges of the surface or with the selected point on the adjacent stamped image.

STAMPING AN ABSTRACT PATTERN

The secret to making an abstract pattern look good is to allow it to bleed off the edges of the surface. If it is confined within the edges, then it will visually conflict with them and look sloppy.

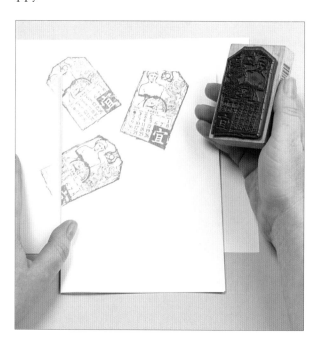

Lay a piece of scrap paper underneath the surface you want to stamp onto (see *Stamping on different surfaces*, pages 38–45). Ink up the stamp (see *Choosing the right medium*, page 33) and press it down onto the surface, allowing part of the stamp to overlap onto the scrap paper. Lift the stamp off cleanly to reveal the stamped design. Continue in this way, building up a pattern of part and whole stamps.

Stamp the image at different angles to enhance the abstract feel.

STAMPING A BORDER

A border stamped up the side of a surface can either balance another single stamp or stand alone. This is another easy technique to perfect.

1 Ink up the stamp (see *Choosing the right medium*, page 33) and position it in the corner of the surface, aligning the edges of the stamp with the corner. Press it down onto the surface (see *Stamping on different surfaces*, pages 38–45).

2 Lift the stamp off cleanly to reveal the stamped design. Re-ink and reposition the stamp, aligning one edge with the edge of the surface and another with the edge of the first stamped image. Continue in this way to stamp the complete border.

If you are stamping a surface that cannot be trimmed to fit a complete number of stamps, start in the middle of the edge. In this way, if a stamp is cut off at the end, it will be cut off equally at both ends, and the border will look symmetrical.

STAMPING A FRAME

You can buy frame stamps in many different sizes and designs, but you might not always be able to find the perfect one. Fortunately, however, stamping your own frame is easy.

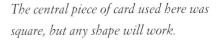

1 Cut a piece of scrap card to the internal size of the frame you want to stamp. Lay this in position on the surface. You can use low-tack spray glue to hold it in place while you stamp.

The central piece of card used here was square, but any shape will work.

2 Ink up the stamp (see *Choosing the right medium*, page 33) and press it down onto the surface (see *Stamping on different surfaces*, pages 38–45). Start at one corner of the frame and align the edge of the stamp backing with the edge of the piece of scrap card. Lift the stamp off cleanly to reveal the stamped design.

3 Repeat the process around the edge of the scrap card, aligning each stamp with the edge of the card and the edge of the previous stamp.

POSITIONING A CENTERPIECE

This technique uses exactly the same principles as positioning a single stamp to perfectly center it within a stamped frame.

Use the stamp positioner as described in *Positioning a single stamp* (see page 47) to stamp a centerpiece within a frame. You may want to measure and make a tiny pencil mark in the exact middle of the frame, to guide you when positioning the flat piece of plastic.

The shape of the frame, and of the central image, does not need to be square for this technique to work.

COLORING A STAMP

Adding color to a stamp is one way of developing it from a simple outline into a picture in its own right. You don't have to be artistic to try these techniques, since you have the outline of the stamp to guide you in applying the color. Some of the techniques give subtle color and shaded effects, while others are bolder, so be sure to choose one that is right for the stamp you are using and complements your project.

WATERCOLOR PENS

Watercolor—or brush—pens can be used with or without water to color in a stamp. Used with water, they allow for shading and subtlety of color. The stamped design must be waterproof, or the outline will run when you wet it.

Used without water, the same pens provide stronger, block color.

With water

By varying the amount of color applied to different sections of the stamp, you can give the stamped image a rounded, three-dimensional look.

1 Scribble some watercolor pens onto a clean plate to make patches of colored ink.

2 Dip a fine paintbrush in water and dilute the colors a bit. Soak the brush in the ink.

3 Stamp a design (see *Paper and card*, page 39). Paint sections of the stamp with the diluted pen inks. If you are painting adjacent sections in different colors, allow one section to dry before painting the next one, to prevent the colors bleeding into one another.

Without water

Watercolor pens are available in a wide range of colors, so you can build up complex designs with them.

Use the fine tip of the watercolor pens to carefully color in sections of the stamp. For a softer, more rustic look, do not apply the color solidly. Scribble delicately with the pen to create broken color.

WATERCOLOR PENCILS

Like watercolor pens, these pencils can be diluted with water to color in a stamp. They are best used with water, though if you apply the color quite densely, they can look effective when dry as well.

By varying the amount of pencil you apply to different sections of the stamp, and using the water to spread the color, you can create subtle shading.

1 Stamp a design (see *Paper and card*, page 39). Either use permanent ink or emboss the stamp to waterproof it. Color in sections or all of the stamp with watercolor pencils.

2 Dip a fine paintbrush in water and use the tip to spread and smooth the color out over the stamp.

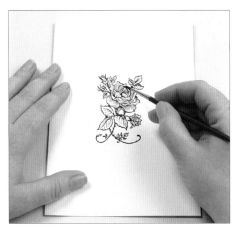

BLENDER PEN

These clever pens have a clear tip that will pick up ink from an ink pad, which you can then use to color in a stamp.

Take advantage of the way the ink fades from the nib of the pen to vary the density of color across the stamp for a more artistic effect.

1 Stamp a design (see *Paper and card*, page 39). Dab the nib of the pen onto an ink pad to pick up some color on the tip.

2 Color in a section of the stamped image, refreshing the color from the pad as needed.

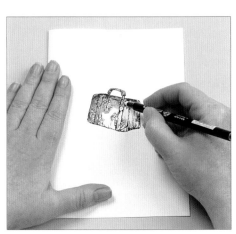

3 To clean the pen between colors, simply scribble it on a piece of scrap paper. The color will quickly leave the pen nib.

WATERCOLOR EFFECT

Both of these techniques offer a way of coloring in a stamp and giving it the look of a watercolor painting. The first technique is simple and requires no artistic ability.

Brush water from the outline inward to avoid spreading color outside the outline.

With pens

1 Color in all the sections of the stamp die with watercolor pens (see *Using brush pens*, page 34).

2 Press the stamp down onto the paper (see *Paper and card*, page 39). Lift it off cleanly to reveal the design.

3 Dip a fine paintbrush into clean water and carefully brush over the stamped image, spreading the color from the outline into the design. Wash the brush between colors.

This technique uses actual watercolor paints. You don't have to be artistic, but a steady hand is necessary to produce the best results.

This technique is suitable for more complex stamps, since the black outline gives the painting shadows and depth.

With paints

1 Ink up the stamp with a permanent ink pad (see *Using ink pads*, page 33) and press it down onto the paper (see *Paper and card*, page 39). Lift it off cleanly to reveal the stamped design. Leave the stamp to dry completely.

2 Using a fine paintbrush, carefully color in the design with watercolor paints. Paint right over the detail in the stamped design.

USING CHALKS

Chalk palettes are available in most craft stores and offer a wide range of colors. Use them to add soft, pretty color to your stamped design.

1 Ink up the stamp with a white pad and press it down onto paper (see *Paper and card*, page 39). Lift it off cleanly to reveal the stamped design. Leave the stamp to dry. The design will be faint, but you should be able to see it well enough to color it in. If you are working on colored paper, choose an ink pad that is the closest possible color match.

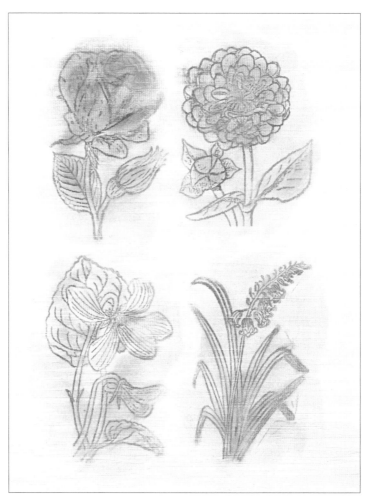

The soft effect this technique gives works well with natural motifs, like these flowers.

2 Rub the tip of a foam cosmetic applicator onto a colored chalk and then gently rub it onto the stamp.

3 Continue to color in the design, using a different side of the applicator—or, if necessary, a fresh applicator—for each new color.

COLORING WITH CHALKS
Here the color has been allowed to bleed over the edges of the stamp to provide a more artistic effect. For a crisper, cleaner finish, work more precisely within the stamped outline.

EMBELLISHING WITH PASTELS

If you have an artistic streak, you will enjoy this technique. The stamped designs will provide a structure for the project, so you can work quite loosely with the pastels to create an impressionistic effect.

This technique works best on a fairly large scale, so consider using it to color a group of stamps.

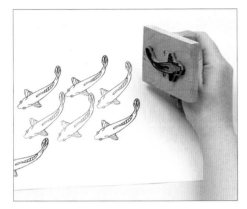

1 Ink up the stamp (see *Choosing the right medium*, page 33) and press it down onto the paper (see *Paper and card*, page 39). Lift it off cleanly to reveal the stamped design. Leave to dry.

2 Color in elements of the design with quite loose strokes of the pastels.

3 Use your finger to smudge the pastels together a little for a softer effect.

4 Color the background making long strokes with the pastels. Again, use your finger to blend the colors together a little.

CREATIVE STAMPING

Once you have mastered the basic stamping techniques, a world of exciting possibilities awaits. You can embellish and decorate stamps in many ways, using simple techniques and interesting products. A range of possibilities is explored in this chapter, from using household objects to stamp with, to gilding, to freehand detailing that really doesn't need much artistic ability to make your projects look good.

STAMPING WITH FOUND OBJECTS

The most unlikely objects can be made into attractive stamps. You just need to use your imagination! Here, pairs of curtain hooks have been used to make a charmingly naive heart stamp.

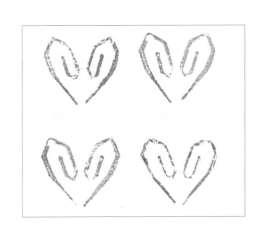

No one would guess that these hearts started out as curtain hooks!

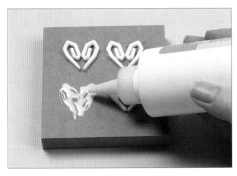

1 Spread some glue on a backboard in roughly the shape of the object that you are going to stick down.

2 Press the object onto the glue and leave to dry. It is a good idea to let it dry facedown so that the stamping surface is as level as possible.

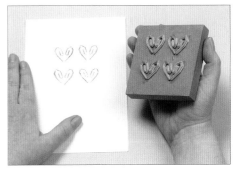

3 Ink up the stamp (see *Choosing the right medium*, page 33) and press it down onto the surface you want to stamp (see *Stamping on different surfaces*, pages 38–45). Lift it off cleanly to reveal the stamped design.

STAMPING WITH METALLIC PAINTS

Gold, copper, bronze, and silver paints can add an interesting extra element to a simple stamp. They work especially well if you use different metallic colors together.

Take the effect further by stamping the metallic paints onto colored metallic paper.

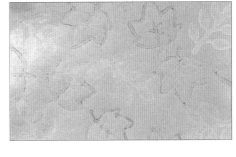

1 Brush metallic paint onto a stamp (see *Brushing a stamp*, page 34).

2 Press the stamp down onto the surface you want to stamp (see *Stamping on different surfaces*, pages 38–45). Lift it off cleanly to reveal the stamped design.

3 Brush another color of metallic paint onto a different stamp, and stamp that design onto the same piece of paper.

DECOUPAGE AND STAMPING

This is a traditional craft that has a large following in its own right. However, it works wonderfully well with stamping and offers an opportunity to combine two crafts to good effect. You can use a single image, as here, or build up layers in cutouts in the traditional way.

Use a single cutout stamp on interesting paper to decorate a greeting card.

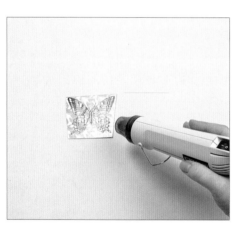

1 Stamp a design onto a piece of paper and emboss it (see *Embossing with powder*, page 75).

2 Using sharp scissors, carefully cut out the embossed stamp.

3 Spray glue onto the back of the cutout stamp.

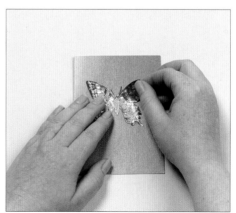

4 Stick the cutout onto a piece of paper or card.

STAMPING WITH GLITTER

This technique is great fun to do with children, but beware, as it can get rather messy. Glitter comes in different weights, and the fine type usually works better than the coarser kind.

1 Brush some craft glue onto a stamp (see *Brushing a stamp*, page 34). Apply the glue quite thickly.

2 Press the stamp down onto the surface you want to stamp (see *Stamping on different surfaces*, pages 38–45). Lift it off cleanly to reveal the sticky shape.

Glitter works best with very bold shapes. If you try to use it on a fine-line stamp, there is a chance that not enough glue will transfer, and thus the glitter will not stick.

3 Sprinkle glitter over the glued area, making sure that it is completely covered.

4 Tip the excess glitter off onto a piece of scrap paper.

5 Use a fine paintbrush to brush off any stray flecks of glitter. Leave to dry. Crease the scrap paper into a scoop and use it to pour the excess glitter back into the pot.

GILDING A STAMP

There are two ways of gilding a stamp. This method produces a motif that can then be mounted onto another surface. It is a useful technique if the surface you want to decorate is not suitable for stamping directly onto.

Use an appropriate adhesive to stick the gilded design to whatever surface you choose.

On self-adhesive film

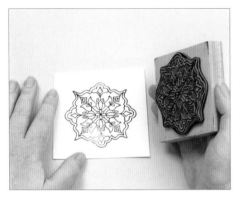

1 Ink up the stamp with an archival ink pad (see *Using ink pads*, page 33) and press it down onto the self-adhesive film. Lift it off cleanly to reveal the stamped design. Leave to dry.

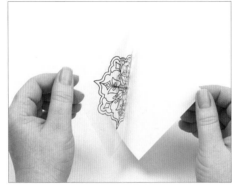

2 Peel the backing off the film and lay it stamped-side down on a flat surface.

3 Position a sheet of metal gilding leaf over the film, and gently lay it down.

4 Use a soft paintbrush to brush the leaf down onto the film, making sure that it is completely adhered.

5 Use your fingers to rub off the excess leaf around the edges of the film.

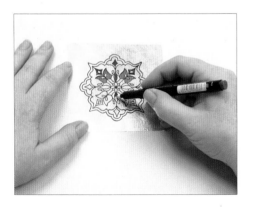

6 Turn the film right-side up. Use projector pens to color in sections of the stamped design. Leave to dry.

7 Using sharp scissors, carefully cut out the design.

On paper

This method of gilding a stamp can be used directly onto the surface you want to decorate. Try using it on different papers, walls, and wood. The leaf is available in various different finishes, including silver, bronze and some special-effect finishes, so choose on to suit your project.

Simple shapes without fine lines work best with this technique.

1 Using a size pen, cover the stamp die with size.

2 Press the stamp down onto the surface you want to decorate (see *Stamping on different surfaces*, pages 38–45). Lift it off cleanly to reveal the stamped design. Following the manufacturer's instructions, leave the glue to become tacky.

3 Position a sheet of metal gilding leaf over the stamped design, and gently lay it down.

4 Use a soft paintbrush to brush the leaf down onto the surface, making sure that all of the size is covered. Leave to dry.

5 Gently brush away any excess leaf.

WORKING WITH METAL LEAF
The leaf is very fragile and very light, so don't handle it roughly, and don't sneeze while you are working! If it tears and some of the size or self-adhesive film shows, just use scrap pieces to patch the hole. It won't show when the design is finished. Save all of the excess leaf in a jar for patching up future projects.

MASKING AND STAMPING

This is a clever technique that allows you to overlap stamped designs, making a number of small images look like one big picture while keeping all the colors separate.

I Stamp the image you want to mask onto a piece of scrap paper. Paper makes a better mask than card, as it will lie completely flat against the surface and you won't get a white "shadow" around the masked image. Cut the image out very carefully, cutting exactly around the edges. The more accurately you cut, the more effective the finished design will look.

2 Spray the back of the cutout mask with low-tack spray glue.

3 Stamp the actual images you want to mask off onto a surface (see *Stamping on different surfaces*, pages 38–45). Leave to dry.

A masked design can be as complex and multilayered as you wish; just mask off more areas.

4 Stick the cutout mask over one of the stamped images. Position the mask accurately so that it completely covers the image underneath.

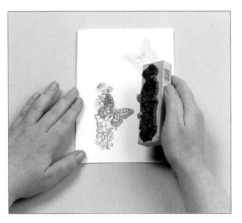

5 Stamp the background image, stamping right over the mask.

6 Carefully peel off the mask. Continue in this way until you have completed the design.

STAMPING WITH MASKING FLUID

Masking fluid works as a resist—it masks off the stamped areas so that you can color the background to produce a negative stamped image. You can either use the results as they are, or cut out sections to use as panels on a project. This would work well if other panels on the project featured positive images made with the same stamp. Use a simple stamp made from foam with this technique.

I Using a cosmetic sponge and a paint pad (see *Making a paint pad*, page 36), dab masking fluid onto a stamp. Dab it on as thickly as possible.

Here, ink pads have been used to color the paper, but you could use paints; just let them dry completely before you start rubbing.

2 Press the stamp down onto the surface (see *Stamping on different surfaces*, pages 38–45). Lift it off cleanly to reveal the stamped design. Leave to dry completely.

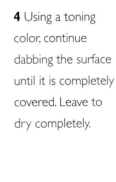

4 Using a toning color, continue dabbing the surface until it is completely covered. Leave to dry completely.

3 Dab over the whole surface with an ink pad, leaving some spaces between the blocks of color.

5 Rub the masked areas with the tip of your finger until the fluid lifts off and peels away. If your finger becomes sore, try wearing a rubber glove.

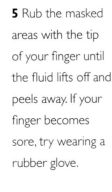

USING ROLLER STAMPS

Roller stamps can be used in a variety of ways, but the most common is as a border or frame. Choose either a complementary or contrasting stamp as the centerpiece.

A border will give a neat finish to a design.

1 Ink up the stamp (see *Choosing the right medium*, page 33) and wheel it onto a scrap piece of paper. Lay this below where you want the actual stamp to be, to act as a guide. Re-ink

the stamp and align the start of the pattern with the starting point on the guide piece. Wheel the stamp smoothly across the paper, keeping a firm, even pressure on the handle. Do not press too hard, or the wheel may slip. Repeat the process on all sides to make a border.

2 Ink up a centerpiece stamp, and stamp it within the border (see *Stamping a centerpiece*, page 51).

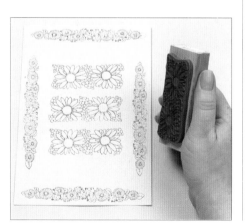

USING PUFFY PAINT

This is an extraordinary paint that is available in most crafts and notions stores. You can use it on a variety of surfaces, and it offers an interesting way of adding texture to a stamp. If you are a glass painter, you will find the piping easy. If not, practice on scrap paper before starting a project.

Because the paint swells when it is heated, it is best not to use it on small or very finely detailed stamps, as the image will become distorted.

1 Stamp a design (see *Paper and card*, page 39). Using the paint straight from the bottle, pipe around the outline of the stamp.

2 Following the manufacturer's instructions, warm the paint with a heat gun until it puffs up.

FREEHAND DETAILING

You don't have to be artistic to embellish a stamp by hand. Some simple lines drawn with a brush pen can turn a plain stamp into a more decorative design.

Freehand detailing is best kept as simple as possible. Experiment with different types of pens, pencils, and crayons to create different effects to complement different stamps.

1 Press a stamp onto a rainbow stamp pad across two stripes so that it picks up different ink colors.

2 Stamp the design onto a piece of paper or card and leave it to dry. Here, a classic flower design has been stamped in an uneven row, and some of the flowers have been allowed to overlap.

3 Use a plastic ruler laid upside down as a guide across the bottom of the paper. Using a brush pen, draw lines down from the base of each flower to the ruler to form stems. Draw shorter lines between them to represent grass.

4 Draw simple leaf shapes sprouting from the flower stems.

5 For a final touch, glue a sequin to the center of some of the flowers (see *Adding sequins*, page 68).

ADDING SEQUINS

Many kinds of circular and shaped sequins are available, and they offer a quick and colorful way of adding extra decoration to a stamped design. Use a glue pen to stick the sequins in place.

1 Stamp the design you want to embellish onto a piece of paper or card (see *Paper and card*, page 39), and leave it to dry.

2 Decide on the position of a sequin and use a glue pen to apply a dot of adhesive in the correct place.

3 Dampen the tip of a finger and pick the sequin up on it. Press the sequin onto the dot of adhesive. Continue until you have applied all the sequins you want. Leave to dry.

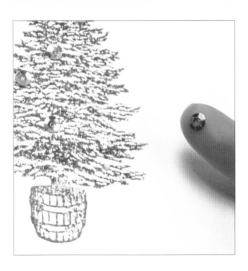

PICKING UP SEQUINS
If you are using very tiny sequins, you may find it easier to dampen the tip of a cocktail stick and pick them up on that.

Some stamps are obvious candidates for this technique; try using it with wreath, flower, and all-over pattern stamps.

DISTRESSING A STAMP

Wood is the best surface to stamp onto if you want to distress the stamp. The effect is very pretty and can be as subtle or as bold as you like, depending on the paint colors you choose and how hard you rub.

The effect is shown here on a picture frame, but it also works beautifully on furniture.

1 Paint the frame with latex paint. Choose a color that complements the original color of the frame, which will show through when you distress the surface.

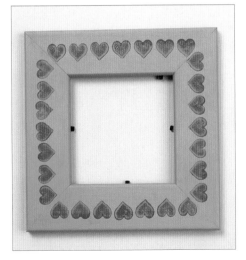

2 Stamp a design onto the frame. Choose a color as close to the original color of the frame as possible. Start stamping in the middle of one side of the frame and work outward to the edges. This way, you will have a balanced number of stamps on each side of the frame.

3 Leave the finished frame to dry completely.

4 Gently rub the frame with a kitchen scourer to take off a layer of paint and reveal the original color. Rub around the inner and outer edges and over some sections of the surface to create a naturally distressed effect.

STAMPING ON FABRIC

Fabrics of many different types can be decorated with stamps. You can embellish dressmaking fabrics and then make them up, or decorate ready-made clothing. You can also stamp furnishing fabrics and make soft furnishings to match or complement other stamped items in a room—a great way to give your room a designer look. When using fabric paints or dyes, always be sure to read and follow the manufacturer's instructions.

STAMPING WITH FABRIC PAINTS

Using a roller

Fabric paints can be purchased at most hobby and craft stores, as well as many notions stores. They can be applied to a stamp in the same way as normal paint.

The textured surface of velvet gives the stamp an appealing, distressed quality.

Using an ink pad

Special paints impregnated into ink pads offer a mess-free way of stamping fabric.

Used with solid stamps, the drier nature of the ink pads gives a broken finish to the stamps.

1 Pour some paint into a dish and use a foam roller to apply it to a stamp (see *Rollering a stamp*, page 35).

2 Press the stamp down onto the fabric, then lift it off cleanly to reveal the stamped design. Leave to dry, then following the manufacturer's instructions, iron the back of the fabric to fix the paint.

1 Ink up the stamp (see *Using ink pads*, page 33).

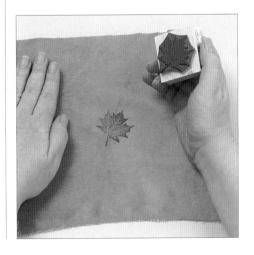

2 Press the stamp down onto the fabric, then lift it off cleanly to reveal the stamped design. Leave to dry, then following the manufacturer's instructions, iron the back of the fabric to fix the paint.

STAMPING WITH FABRIC PENS

Fabric pens are great for stamping, since they allow you to color different sections of a stamp to produce a multicolored image.

Since the pens dry quite quickly, they are best used with small stamps.

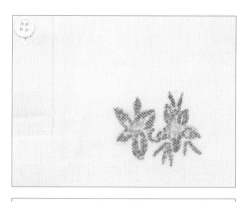

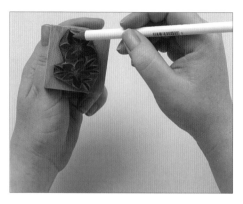

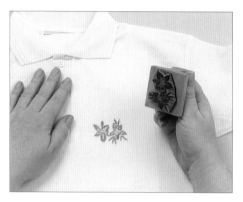

USING FABRIC PENS

If the fabric slips on the paper when you are stamping, use a sheet of fine sandpaper instead of the paper. The sandpaper will grip the fabric and help to hold it in place.

I Color the stamp with the pens (see *Using brush pens*, page 34). Lay a piece of paper under the fabric on which you are stamping to prevent the color bleeding through onto other layers of fabric.

2 Press the stamp down onto the fabric, then lift it off cleanly to reveal the design. Leave to dry, then following the manufacturer's instructions, iron the back of the fabric to fix the paint.

EMBOSSING VELVET

This is a wonderful way of producing subtle, luxurious embossed designs. It works only on fabrics with a pile, and because the iron needs to be quite hot, it is better to avoid synthetics.

Quite detailed stamps reproduce well with this technique, though small, very fine stamps won't work.

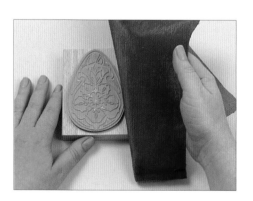

I Lay the stamp on its back, and lay the fabric pile-side down over it.

2 Lay a piece of kitchen paper over the back of the fabric. Set the iron to a hot setting and press it down onto the kitchen paper. Don't move the iron at all for approximately 30 seconds.

3 Remove the paper and then peel the fabric off the stamp to reveal the embossed design.

STAMPING BATIK

Stamping can be used in conjunction with the traditional craft of batik to produce personalized fabrics. The technique works best with bolder stamps, since painting the wax thickly enough onto fine lines is quite difficult.

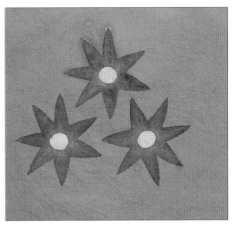

Try making soft furnishings from stamped batik fabric to complement a stamped wall (see Stamping on walls, *page 40).*

I Stamp onto the fabric with fabric paints (see *Stamping with fabric paints*, page 71). Leave it to dry, then following the manufacturer's instructions, iron the fabric on the back to fix the color.

2 Melt the batik wax following the manufacturer's instructions. Using a soft paintbrush, paint over the stamped design with the wax. Paint the wax on quite thickly so that it soaks right through the fabric. If necessary, paint more wax onto the back of the design to ensure that it penetrates the fabric.

MAKING THE MOST OF COLORS
As well as the colors of the fabric paint and the dye, you also have the original color of the fabric at your disposal. Painting the wax onto the original fabric color will make that part resistant to the the dye. Here, the centers of the flowers are the original fabric color.

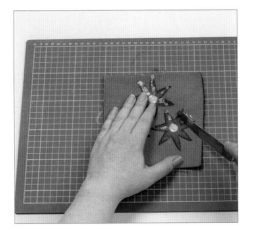

3 Again following the manufacturer's instructions, mix up some cold-water dye. Dip the fabric in and leave it for the stated time. Remove the fabric and rinse it several times to remove any excess dye. Leave the fabric to dry naturally.

4 Lay the fabric on a cutting mat and, using the blade of a table knife, scrape away as much wax as possible.

5 Place the fabric between sheets of tissue paper and iron it to remove the last traces of the wax.

EMBOSSED EFFECTS

Traditional embossing involves using a heavy press and engraved metal plates to press an image into paper, but fortunately today there are simpler ways of creating an embossed effect. You are also not limited to paper; wax, polymer clay, and metal foil, as well as many kinds of paper and card, can also be embossed using the simple techniques shown in this chapter.

EMBOSSING WITH POWDER

This is a very simple technique that gives spectacular results. It is not only decorative in itself but also provides a basis for other techniques, since it makes the stamped outline waterproof, which is useful if you are coloring in the design.

Embossing with powder can be used to produce subtle images, as above, or vibrant effects if the powder contrasts with the background.

1 Ink up the stamp with an embossing ink pad (see *Using ink pads*, page 33) and press it down onto the surface you want to stamp (see *Stamping on different surfaces*, pages 38–45). Lift it off cleanly to reveal the stamped design.

USING COLORED INK PADS
You can use pigment ink pads for embossing. Dye ink pads, however, are not suitable, since you have to work very fast to apply the embossing powder before the ink dries.

2 Working quickly while the ink is still wet, sprinkle some embossing powder over the whole design.

3 Tip the excess powder off onto a sheet of scrap paper. Use the paper as a scoop to pour the powder back into the pot to be used again.

4 Using a fine paintbrush, carefully brush away any grains of powder clinging to the paper outside the stamped design.

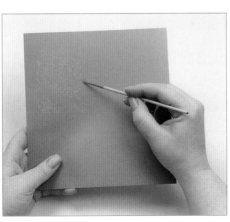

5 Following the instructions, warm the powder with a heat gun until it fuses. Do not overheat the powder. Once it has fused together, do not continue heating it.

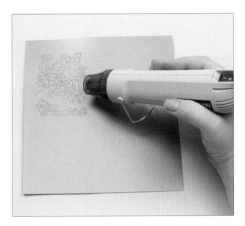

EMBOSSING ONTO SCRAPER BOARD

Traditional scraper board works well with embossing. The texture of the scraped areas contrasts effectively with the smooth surface of the board and the embossed stamp.

The embossed area can be cut out and mounted on a card as a decorative panel.

1 Emboss a stamp onto scraper board (see *Embossing with powder*, page 75).

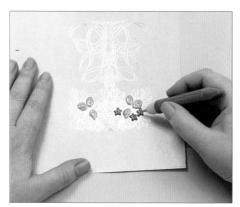

2 Using a scraper tool or a metal nail file, carefully scrape away areas within the stamped design.

BUYING SCRAPER BOARD
Scraper board has a matte surface that is scraped away to reveal the colored background underneath. It can be bought in most craft stores in a variety of colors, including gold, silver, copper, white, rainbow, and a holographic finish.

USING THREE-DIMENSIONAL PAINTS

These paints work well with stamps. They are sold in soft plastic tubes that have a fine nozzle, allowing you to apply fine detail straight from the tube. The raised outline is quite shallow, giving a finish that is embossed and colored at the same time.

USING GLASS PAINTING OUTLINER
Gold, silver, or even black glass painting outliner can also be used in the same way to give an embossed effect.

Depending on your skill with the paints, you can use this technique on highly detailed stamps.

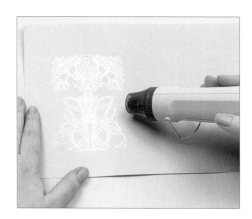

1 Emboss a stamp onto paper (see *Embossing with powder*, page 75).

2 Using the paint straight from the tube, start filling in sections of the stamp. Let one section dry before working on an adjacent one, to prevent the colors bleeding into one another. Use short strokes to fill in the more detailed sections.

3 On longer sections, try to fill in a whole section with one continuous line of paint for the smoothest effect.

STAMPING ONTO WAX

Sealing wax gives a decorative touch to a special letter or card. Traditionally the seal was stamped with a signet ring, but any metal stamp will work.

Sealing wax

1 Warm the sealing wax over a candle, turning the stick of wax constantly in the flame until it is just about to drip. Blow out the candle as soon as you have finished, and never leave a burning candle unattended.

Choose a stamp appropriate to complement the letter you are sending—a sunny greeting to a friend, for example.

2 Drip some wax onto the flap of the envelope. If you are posting it, seal it in the usual way first.

3 While the wax is still soft, press the stamp into it. Lift the stamp off cleanly to reveal the design.

COLORING THE SEAL
You can add a further decorative touch by spreading a little gold rubbing wax over the seal. Gold works well with red, but if you are using another color of sealing wax, experiment with other colors of rubbing wax to suit.

Candle wax

Stamping is a neat way to decorate a plain candle, turning it into a decorative feature.

Choose a simple solid shape to stamp with, since fine details won't show up very well.

1 Warm the candle with a heat gun until the wax is soft but not dripping.

2 While the wax is still soft, press the stamp into it. Press hard, then lift the stamp off cleanly to reveal the design.

STAMPING ONTO POLYMER CLAY

Polymer clay is a popular medium, which also works well with stamps. The results can be used to make such items as Christmas decorations, refrigerator magnets, and jewelry.

Colorful and easy to use, polymer clay is an ideal material for children to stamp onto.

1 Roll out the clay on a piece of grease-proof paper. Here, a tube of paint has been used as a small rolling pin.

2 Press a stamp into the clay. Do not press too hard, and lift the stamp off cleanly to reveal the design.

3 Use a cookie cutter to stamp out a shape in the clay. Remember to check that the cutter is larger than the stamp!

5 Use a pointed tool to make a hole in the clay if you wish to hang the finished item. Following the manufacturer's instructions, bake the clay in the oven until it is hard.

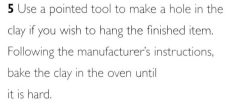

4 Gently slip the clay shape out of the stamp.

EMBOSSING METAL FOIL

Embossed foil can look wonderfully glamorous and adds a special touch to a project. It is widely available in several metal finishes.

The finished item can be mounted onto a card or even onto a wall.

1 Ink up the stamp with a permanent ink pad (see *Using ink pads*, page 33) and press it down onto the foil. Lift it off cleanly to reveal the stamped design. Leave to dry.

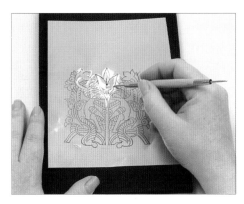

2 Lay the foil on an embossing mat: a computer mouse pad or a wad of folded newspaper will work equally well. Using an embossing tool or a dried-up ballpoint pen, draw over all the stamped lines, pressing firmly onto the foil.

3 When you have finished, turn the foil over to check that the design is complete.

4 Using sharp scissors, carefully cut out the embossed shape. Cut as close as possible to the outer embossed lines.

5 Stick self-adhesive pads to the back of the metal shape. Peel off the paper backings.

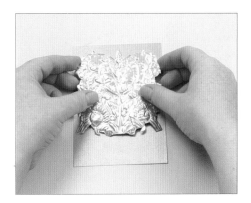

6 Lay the metal shape onto a card and very gently press it in place. Do not press too hard, or you will mark the foil.

THREE-DIMENSIONAL EFFECTS

You can add extra interest to stamped designs by introducing depth. This can be done physically by layering or punching stamps— or visually with shadow stamping. You could even try combining techniques to further enhance the effects by punching sections out of shadow or concentric stamps before layering them.

STAMPING AND PUNCHING

Hobby punches are available in a wide range of shapes, many of which complement stamps. Because most punches do not have a long reach, this technique is best used on narrow strips of paper. There are special long-reach punches available, but the designs are limited.

As well as using the pieces punched out of the stamps, punch other pieces out of plain paper and use these to embellish the stamped design, too.

1 Stamp a row of shapes onto a strip of paper and leave them to dry.

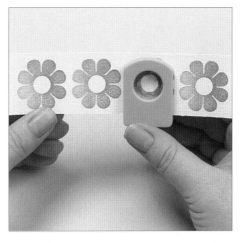

2 Turn the punch upside down and slide the stamped paper into it. Position the paper so that you are punching out a suitable section of some of the stamps, and punch out as many shapes as you need.

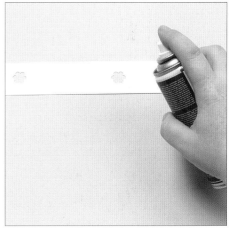

3 Spray glue onto the back of the stamped strip of paper and stick it onto a piece of complementary-colored paper.

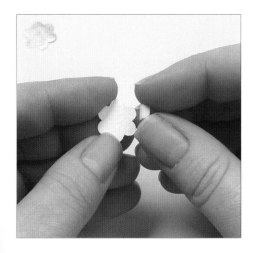

4 Stick an adhesive pad to the back of each punched-out piece of paper.

5 Stick the punched-out shapes onto elements of the stamped design.

LAYERED STAMPS

For this technique you need a stamp that has a concentric design, so that you can cut it out in different sizes. You need at least three layers to produce a good effect.

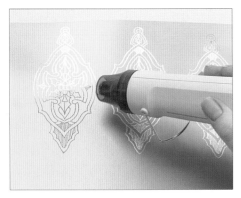

I Emboss a stamp onto card (see *Embossing with powder*, page 75).

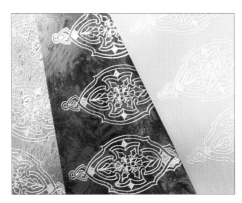

2 Emboss the same stamp several times onto three different colors of card; here, matte gold, black, and shiny gold have been used.

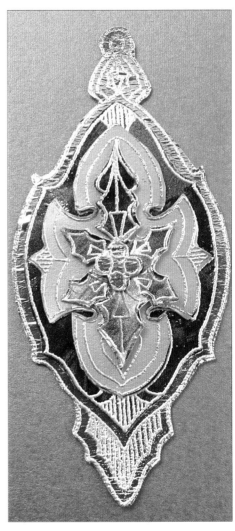

The finished layered design works well as a decorative panel on the front of a card.

3 First, cut the whole stamp out of one color of card. Use sharp scissors and cut as close to the embossed outline as possible.

4 On a separate stamp, cut out the next concentric outline. This may be a different shape to the first outline, but this doesn't matter as long as it is the next size down.

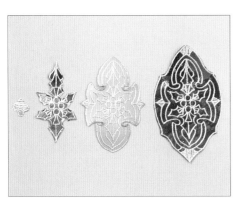

5 Cut out as many concentric shapes as the stamped design will allow. Ensure that each successive shape is in a different color so that they stand out well.

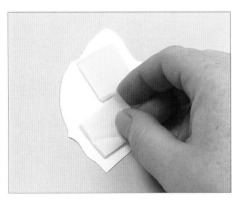

6 Stick self-adhesive pads to the back of each cutout shape. For the smallest shapes, cut the pads down to size with scissors.

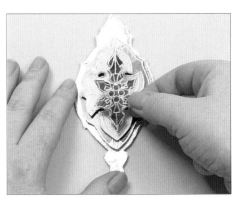

7 Peel the paper backings off the pads and carefully stick the shapes one on top of another. Line each one up so that it is sitting centrally on top of the one below.

SHADOW STAMPING

A subtle technique, shadow stamping relies on contrasts between color and tone for the best effects. You can buy special shadow stamps in craft stores, or you can make your own background stamps from sponge.

1 Using a light color, ink up a block stamp with a pale ink pad (see *Using ink pads*, page 33), and press it down onto the paper (see *Paper and card*, page 39). Lift it off cleanly to reveal the stamped rectangle.

Keep shadow-stamped designs fairly simple. They don't need to be complex to be effective.

2 Using a different-sized block stamp, stamp another overlapping rectangle in a different pale color. Continue stamping to build up a background. Leave to dry.

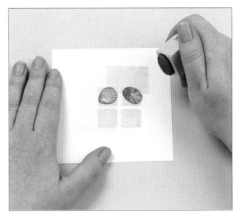

3 Ink up an outline rubber stamp with a strong color, and stamp onto the background. Position the stamp sensitively on the rectangles.

EDIBLE STAMPING

What a great way to decorate cakes and cookies! The techniques shown here were done on sugar paste, but cookies can also be colored with edible ink pens or food coloring. Raw cookie dough can be embossed with a stamp; it is best to use a stamp with a strong outline since the baking process can blur the image. Be sure never to decorate food with nonedible paints.

EMBOSSING SUGAR PASTE

Simple but sophisticated, embossed sugar paste can be used to great effect on wedding and Christmas cakes.

With a single stamp

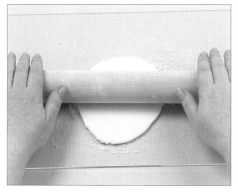

1 Roll out the sugar paste on a marble board or a piece of thick plastic. Do not roll it too thin. Sprinkle some icing sugar on the board and rolling pin to stop the sugar paste sticking.

2 Press the stamp firmly into the paste. Lift it off cleanly to reveal the stamped design.

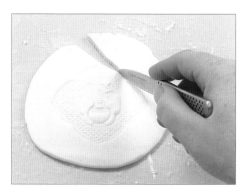

3 Carefully cut around the design, cutting as close to the stamped edges as possible.

The embossed panel can be applied to a frosted cake by dampening the back and gently pressing it in place.

COLORING A STAMP
Edible powders can be bought in various colors from specialty food stores. Use them to add color to an embossed panel. Just brush them on to the sugar paste with a clean, soft paintbrush.

With a roller stamp

Use this technique to make "lace" to trim the edges of a special cake.

This lace pattern works well, but do experiment with other wheel stamps: A trail of paw prints, for example, would look good running around a child's birthday cake.

1 Roll out the icing as before. Run a wheel stamp over the surface, pressing down firmly.

2 Carefully cut out the "lace," cutting as close as possible to the stamped edges.

USING EDIBLE INKS

Stamping is a great way to add decoration to a cake or to cookies. Edible ink pens are available in craft stores and in many specialty food stores.

This sugar-paste circle has been stamped with a design and can now be applied to a cake.

With pens

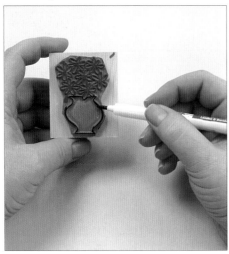

1 Use edible ink pens to color the stamp (see *Using brush pens*, page 34).

2 Press the stamp onto the sugar paste. Do not press too hard, and hold the stamp in place for a few seconds to let the color transfer. Lift the stamp off cleanly to reveal the design.

On embossed paste

You can also use edible pens to color in an embossed design.

This technique works well when the colored designs are mixed with embossed-only designs made with the same stamp.

Emboss a piece of sugar paste with a stamp (see *Embossing sugar paste*, page 85). Use the edible inks to draw over the stamped lines to add color to the design.

USING FOOD COLORING

Ordinary food coloring provides another way of applying decoration to cakes with stamps. Food coloring is widely available, but usually only in a limited range of colors. Make the most of this by using just one or two colors to create graphic decorations.

You can use tints of a color by stamping twice without re-inking the stamp in between. The second stamp will be paler than the first one.

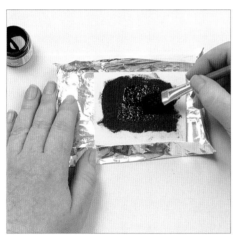

1 Make up a paint pad (see *Making a paint pad*, page 36) and brush some food coloring onto it.

2 Press the stamp down onto the food coloring.

3 Press the stamp gently onto the sugar paste, then lift it off cleanly to reveal the stamped design.

DECORATING A CAKE

The edible stamping techniques shown here have all been demonstrated on circles of sugar paste, and this is certainly the best cake-decorating medium to use with stamping. The circles can be attached to a frosted cake by brushing a little cold water onto the back of them and then simply laying them in position. Working on separate pieces of sugar paste—rather than directly onto a frosted cake—is a good idea; if you make a mistake, you only have to throw away the piece, not re-ice the whole cake.

THE PROJECTS

Having experimented with different stamping techniques, it is now time to start developing your ideas into projects. To start you off and to inspire you to make your own unique pieces, we have created a series of projects in a range of different styles and for different occasions. Here you will find projects for the home, party ideas,

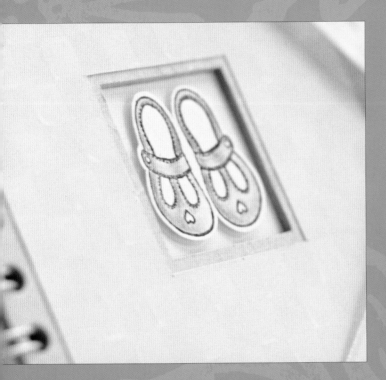

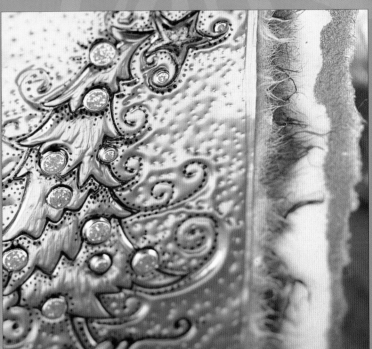

gifts for family and friends, heirloom items and keepsakes to treasure, and greeting cards and personalized stationery. All of the projects use techniques explained in the first section of the book, combining them and developing them further to show you new ways to make the most of your stamping adventure.

"BABY MEMORIES" SCRAPBOOK COVER

Welcome a new baby with a scrapbook made just for him or her. This book has been made in blue for a little boy, but it would work just as well in pink, lemon, or any other pretty pastel shade.

MATERIALS

White paint

Paintbrush

Gingham stamp

Pale blue paper

Pencil

Steel rule

Craft knife

Cutting mat

Hardcover scrapbook

Paper adhesive

Double-sided tape

Gingham ribbon

Baby shoes stamp

Mid-blue ink pad

White paper

Pale blue
watercolor pencil

Sharp scissors

Self-adhesive pad

TECHNIQUES

Choosing a stamp,
pages 28–31

Using ink pads, page 33

Brushing a stamp, page 34

Paper and card, page 39

Stamping a repeat pattern,
page 49

Watercolor pencils,
page 54

The techniques shown here could be used to make a cover for almost any themed scrapbook. A background pattern of hearts and a central dove, for example, would work well for a wedding book.

1 Brush white paint onto the gingham stamp and stamp onto the pale blue paper. Stamp as many times as needed to cover the paper, matching the pattern repeat carefully.

3 Again cutting along the lines of the gingham pattern, cut a central aperture in the paper, large enough to comfortably hold the baby shoes stamp design.

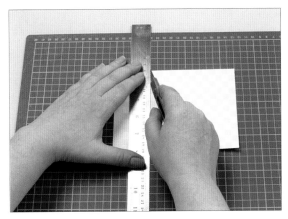

2 Cutting along the lines of the gingham pattern, cut out a square of paper large enough to fit the front of the scrapbook. Use the craft knife and steel rule on the cutting mat.

4 Using paper adhesive, stick the gingham square centrally to the front of the book.

5 Mark a square on the front cover of the book, just inside the gingham square. Using the craft knife and steel rule, cut out the marked square.

(continued)

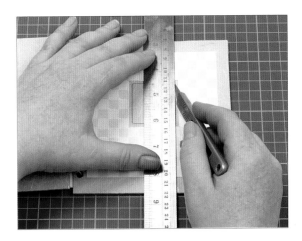

"BABY MEMORIES" SCRAPBOOK COVER *(continued)*

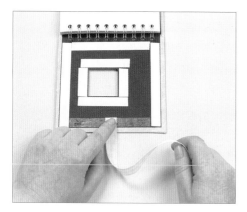

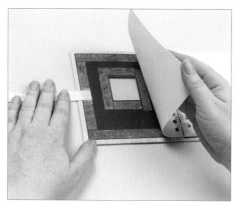

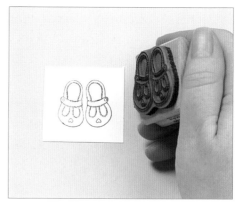

6 Open the front cover of the book and stick lengths of double-sided tape around the outer edge and around the edge of the aperture. Peel the paper backing off the length on the front edge and stick one end of a piece of ribbon to it.

7 Stick a strip of double-sided tape over the end of the ribbon. Peel the paper backing off all of the tape. Stick the first page of the book to the inside of the front cover, smoothing it down. Repeat the process on the back cover with another piece of ribbon.

8 Ink up the baby shoes stamp with the mid-blue ink pad and stamp onto the white paper.

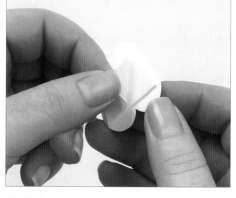

9 Use the pale blue watercolor pencil to color in the stamped design.

10 Using sharp scissors, carefully cut out the shoes, leaving a narrow border of white paper all around them.

11 Stick an adhesive pad to the back of the stamped shoes.

12 Stick the shoes in the center of the aperture in the front of the book. The shoes should not sit higher than the cover, or they will get damaged. if necessary, cut the self-adhesive pad down to suit.

CARD WITH TAG AND GIFT WRAP

Two different embossing techniques are used to make this textural holiday greeting card. The gleaming foil is in high relief, and the gold powder in low relief.

(continued)

Stamp and emboss green mulberry paper with gold trees to make gift wrap to match the greeting card. To complete the look, make a miniature version of the card, using just a section of the stamp, as a gift tag.

CARD WITH TAG AND GIFT WRAP *(continued)*

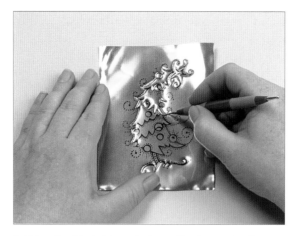

1 Using the black ink pad, stamp the tree onto the metal foil. Remember to clean the stamp immediately. Leave the ink to dry completely. Working on the stamped side of the foil, draw over all the lines with the thin end of the embossing tool.

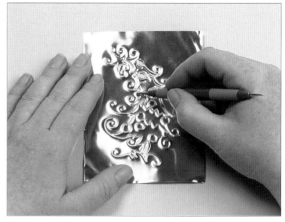

2 Turn the foil over and, using the thick end of the tool, work into the inside sections of the tree. This pushes them the other way, so that they stand out on the right side. Start by working along the edges of the lines embossed in Step 1, then work across the sections. You can make embossed lines to suit the shape of design of the stamp you have used. Here, short vertical lines are used to represent the needles on the tree.

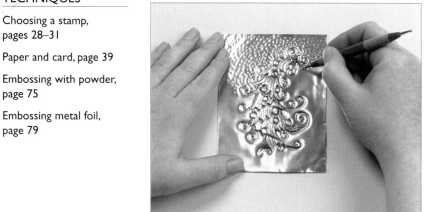

3 Working on the stamped side, press the thin end of the tool into the foil around the tree to create a pattern of dots, giving a beaten metal look. You can work the dots in lines or swirls to complement the shape of the stamp.

4 Stick a diamond dot onto each of the raised baubles on the tree.

5 Using double-sided tape, stick the foil to the piece of white mulberry paper. Draw a line around the foil with a wet paintbrush and tear the paper. Pull out fibers to make a fringe (see Steps 2 and 3 of *Retro picture frame*, page 118). Repeat the process with the green mulberry paper to make a double mount.

6 Using the gold ink pad and embossing powder, emboss some trees onto vellum. Tear a strip of the embossed vellum approximately 1¼ inches (3 cm) wide. Spray the back with glue and stick it to the left-hand side of the card, close to the fold.

7 Stick double-sided tape to the back of the foil panel. Peel off the paper backing and stick the panel to the card, just overlapping the edge of the vellum.

8 Tear a narrow strip off the front and back edges of the card (see Step 3 of *Halloween card and bag*, page 107).

9 Dab clear adhesive onto the torn edges and sprinkle on gold embossing powder. Use a heat gun to melt the powder. The thicker the glue you use, the more textured the embossing will be since the glue bubbles when heated.

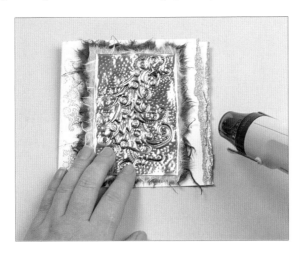

ART NOUVEAU MIRROR

Surprisingly simple to make, this project can easily be adapted to fit any shape or size of mirror. The shape of the mirror and frame should complement the shape of the stamp. So if you want to use a long, thin stamp, choose a narrow rectangular frame and mirror.

MATERIALS

Box picture frame with mount

Art nouveau stamp

Permanent black ink pad

Household scissors

⅛ inch- (3 mm-) wide self-adhesive lead

Boning tool

Craft knife

Piece of mirror cut to fit the frame. (This should not be too tight a fit or you may break it when fitting it.)

Pen

Pale green vellum

Clear paper adhesive

TECHNIQUES

Choosing a stamp, pages 28–31

Using ink pads, page 33

Paper and card, page 39

Glass, page 42

Positioning a single stamp, page 47

Simple and stylish, this mirror would be equally at home in a traditional or modern home.

1 Take the box frame apart. Lay the glass in position over the picture mount and stamp onto it twice, positioning the stamps so that they overlap the inner edge of the mount.

2 Using the scissors, cut two lengths of lead slightly longer than the sides of the stamp. Stick one length down along two opposite sides of the stamp. When sticking the lead, hold one end down in position and gently pull the lead straight with your other hand, then stick it down.

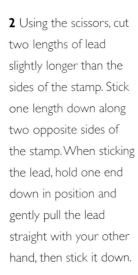

3 Stick longer lengths of lead along the other two sides of the stamp. These lengths should run off one side of the glass.

(continued)

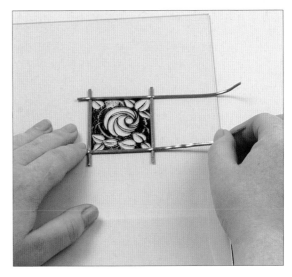

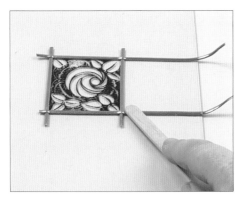

4 Use the boning tool or a wooden clothes peg to rub the lead down onto the glass. Concentrate particularly around the overlaps so that they are well stuck down.

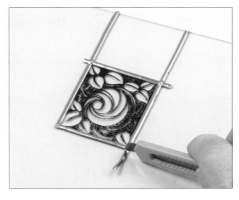

5 Use the craft knife to cut off the protruding ends. Lead the other stamp in the same way.

6 Lay the mount over the mirror glass and mark its position with temporary pen marks. Stamp once onto the mirror, positioning the stamp so that it will lie partly under the mount. Lead it in the same way as the stamps on the glass.

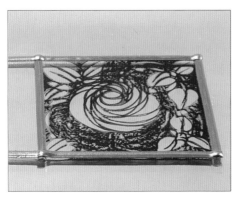

7 The finished stamps should look like this.

8 Stamp four times onto the green vellum and leave to dry.

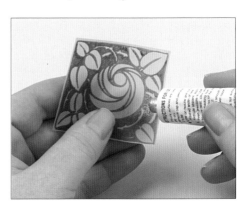

9 Cut out the stamps and put a little clear glue on the back of each one. Put the glue on the stamped areas so that it doesn't show on the front.

10 Stick one square onto each corner of the mount. Align a corner of the square with an inner corner of the mount.

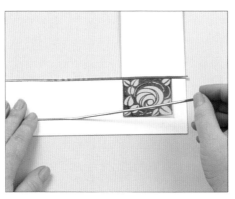

11 Stick four long lengths of lead right across the mount in one direction, aligning them with the edges of the squares. Rub the lead down, and trim the ends as before.

12 Stick down four more lengths, running in the opposite direction and aligning with the other edges of the squares. Reassemble the frame.

VINE AND LEAF BORDER

Simple to make, this vine and leaf border can easily be adapted to complement any room decor. Choose stamps and paint colors that are compatible with the existing furnishings in the room. Consider stamping fabric to make soft furnishings to tie in with the border. Note that you will need to position the stamps carefully for the best effect.

MATERIALS

Plain paper dado border

Scrap paper

Brayer

Paints in four toning colors

Curly vine stamp

Three leaf stamps

Tape measure

Pencil

Spirit level

Wallpaper paste

TECHNIQUES

Choosing a stamp,
pages 28-31

Rollering a stamp, page 35

Paper and card, page 39

Stamping an abstract
pattern, page 50

Stamping a border would be a perfect way to complement other stamped designs in a room scheme.

1 Lay the border out on the scrap paper. Roller paint onto the vine stamp and stamp the border quite densely, allowing some of the stamps to overlap the edges of the paper.

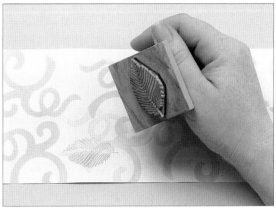

2 Roller one leaf stamp with a different-colored paint, and over stamp the vines. Space the leaves widely, leaving room for the leaves to come.

HANGING THE BORDER

Mark the position of the border on the wall. Use a spirit level to draw a straight line along the wall at this height. Paste the back of the strip, ensuring that you do not get it too wet. Hang the strip at the marked height.

3 Repeat the process with the second leaf stamp in a third color, stamping between the first leaves. Keep standing back from your work to ensure that you are spacing the leaves regularly along the border.

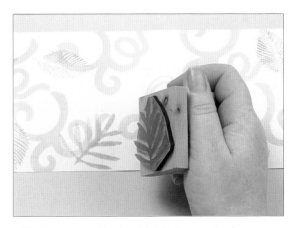

4 Finally, stamp with the third leaf stamp in the remaining color. Consider the placing of each leaf so that the final border design is well balanced.

MATERIALS

Cream blank card

Large outline heart stamp

Deep red ink pad

Deep red
embossing powder

Heat gun

Craft knife

Cutting mat

Love letter
montage stamp

Gold ink pad

Tissue

Single heart stamp

Double-sided tape

Piece of gold vellum 1/16
inch (2 mm) smaller all
around than the blank
card opened-out

TECHNIQUES

Choosing a stamp,
pages 28–31

Paper and card, page 39

Positioning a single stamp,
page 47

Stamping an abstract
pattern, page 50

Stamping a border, page
50

Embossing with powder,
page 75

VALENTINE CARD

Romance is definitely in the air with this pretty, nostalgic Valentine card. A combination of deep red and gold inks on a cream card, together with layered images, lend a traditional feel, reminiscent of Victorian découpage.

1 Stamp two outline hearts onto the front of a folded card with red ink. Sprinkle embossing powder over them and emboss them with the heat gun.

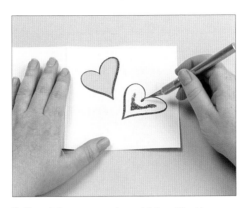

2 Carefully cut out the middle of both hearts with the craft knife. Cut just inside the embossed outline.

3 Use the montage stamp to stamp a background pattern over the front of the card in gold ink. Lay paper underneath the card front and over the back panel so that you can stamp over the edges. Stamp right over the embossed hearts.

4 Use the tissue to wipe any traces of the gold background paint off the embossed hearts. Wrap the tissue around the tip of a finger and wipe from the inside edges.

5 Using deep red ink and the single heart stamp, stamp segments of a border around the edges of the card. Leave to dry.

6 Open the card out flat and stick a short piece of double-sided tape to the back, just to the right of the score line. Position the piece of tape centrally and peel off the paper backing.

7 Fold the piece of vellum in half lengthwise. Hold the front of the card up at right angles to the back. Align the fold in the vellum with the fold of the card and position the vellum so that it sits centrally in the card. Press it down onto the tape. Open the card and vellum out flat and press the vellum firmly onto the tape.

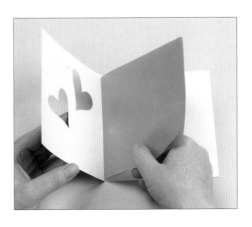

The same principle of using a cutout front and colored internal sheet could be used to make other cards. Try a Christmas card with a cutout tree and green internal sheet.

EMBELLISHED FAMILY TREE

A perfect gift to celebrate the arrival of a new member of the family, a wedding or a special anniversary, a family tree is also a fun project to make. It can be as large and as complicated—including cousins, aunts, and nephews—or as simple as you want it to be.

Stamped and embossed flowers can be added to the petals of some flowers for a finishing touch.

MATERIALS

Computer and printer

Cream paper

Scissors

Cosmetic sponge

Yellow ink pad

Decorative-edge scissors

Scrap paper

Large sheet of
yellow paper

Large floral pattern stamp

Clear embossing ink pad

White embossing powder

Brush pens

Picture frame with mount

Tracing paper

Pencil

Self-adhesive pads

Double-sided tape

Large single-flower stamp

White and ivory papers

All-purpose adhesive

TECHNIQUES

Choosing a stamp,
pages 28–31

Paper and card, page 39

Watercolor pens, page 53

Decoupage and stamping,
page 60

Freehand detailing,
page 67

Embossing with powder,
page 75

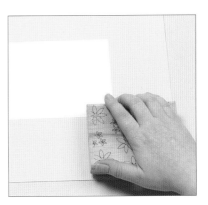

1 Print out the family's names from a computer onto cream paper. Cut out rectangles with the individual's or couple's names on each one. Dab a cosmetic sponge onto the ink pad and gently rub the color onto the edges of the paper. Leave to dry.

2 Cut scalloped edges around each rectangle with decorative scissors. Ensure that you cut within the yellow border.

3 To emboss a border, cut a mask from scrap paper, large enough to contain the family tree. Position the mask on the yellow paper. Using clear embossing ink, stamp around the mask with the large floral pattern stamp. Emboss the stamps.

4 Use brush pens to color some elements of some of the flowers.

5 Lay the mount over the embossed paper and arrange the names within it. Lay a sheet of tracing paper over the area and draw pencil lines connecting the family members. Remove the names and trace the lines onto the paper. Draw over the traced lines with a brown brush pen.

6 Stick self-adhesive pads to the back of each name and stick them in place on the paper. Stick strips of double-sided tape to the back inner edges of the mount and stick the paper into it.

7 Emboss some white flowers onto the white and ivory papers. Use the large flower stamp and the pattern stamp and cut some individual flowers out of the pattern. Cut out all the flower shapes and color some, as in Step 5. Use adhesive to stick some flowers to the top left and bottom right corners of the mount. A few tiny flowers can be used to decorate some of the names.

EMBELLISHED FAMILY TREE ❀ **103**

DECORATED CAKE

Stamps and edible powders can turn a plain cake into a culinary creation fit for any occasion. The subtle shading of the edible powders can be created in a color scheme to suit the occasion, or for a wedding the embossing could be left white and just dusted with white powder to give it sparkle.

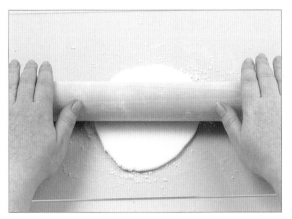

1 Dust the board with some icing sugar and roll out a piece of sugar paste.

2 Stamp onto the paste with the large oval stamp.

3 Cut out the embossed design with a knife. Repeat the process to make seven stamped ovals.

4 Brush a little red powder onto the center of each oval.

5 Brush bronze powder around the red, blending the colors together where they meet.

6 Brush gold powder onto the rest of the oval, again blending the colors.

You could use the same principles to decorate a host of cupcakes for a colorful teatime treat.

MATERIALS

Piece of thick plastic or marble rolling board

Icing sugar

Sugar paste

Rolling pin

Large oval stamp

Sharp knife

Red, bronze, gold, and white edible powders

Fine paintbrush

Water

Cake iced with sugar paste

TECHNIQUES

Choosing a stamp, pages 28–31

Embossing sugar paste, page 85

(continued)

DECORATED CAKE *(continued)*

7 Finally, brush white luster powder over the whole oval, softening and further blending the colors.

8 The finished sugar paste ovals should look like this.

9 Roll out another piece of paste and stamp it twice with the same stamp. Cut out one central flower and the center section of the other one.

10 Color the flowers with powders in the same way as the ovals.

11 Brush a little water onto the back of each oval.

12 Position the first oval on the cake, allowing it to bend over the edge at one end.

13 Position the other ovals around the cake, as shown.

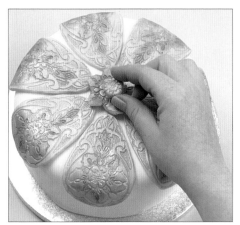

14 Place the flower in the center of the cake. Lay the cutout section on top of it.

HALLOWEEN CARD AND BAG

Celebrate Halloween in style with a bewitched card and matching trick-or-treat bag. Both are simple to make from textured paper and stamps but when finished have a really professional look.

MATERIALS

Small orange ink pad

White blank card

Scrap paper

Spider stamp

Black ink pad

Haunted-house stamp

Black glitter embossing powder

Heat gun

Embossing pen

Paper adhesive

Black mulberry paper

Fine paintbrush

Water

Sheet of black mulberry paper and sheet of white-and-gold gossamer paper

Double-sided tape

Empty box

Paper hole punch

36-inch (90-cm) cord

Piece of stiff card

White card

TECHNIQUES

Choosing a stamp, pages 28–31

Paper and card, page 39

Positioning a single stamp, page 47

Stamping an abstract pattern, page 50

Embossing with powder, page 75

(continued)

Make several cards as invitations to a Halloween party, or just one for a special friend.

The card

I Use the small orange ink pad to stamp squares directly onto the front of the card. Lay the scrap paper underneath so that you can stamp over the edges.

2 Stamp a black spider onto each square, allowing them to crawl over the edges a little.

3 Stamp and then emboss the haunted house onto a piece of smooth card. Use the black ink and black glitter powder. Tear the card into a square around the stamp. As you tear, pull the excess paper toward you so that the torn edge is on the front of the square.

4 Dab around the torn edges of the square with an embossing pen. Sprinkle on embossing powder and heat it until it melts.

5 Using paper adhesive, stick the paper square to a piece of the mulberry paper. Paint a line of water around the edge of the square and tear it out. Pull the fibers out carefully to make a ragged edge (see Steps 2 and 3 of *Retro picture frame*, page 118).

6 Stick the whole panel to the stamped card with the paper adhesive.

The bag

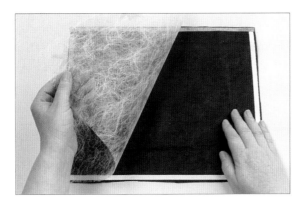

1 Stick lengths of double-sided tape around the edges of the sheet of mulberry paper as close to the edges as possible. Peel the backing paper off the tape and lay the sheet of gossamer paper over the top. Smooth it down carefully, ensuring that you do not make any wrinkles.

2 Stick a length of double-sided tape along one short side of the mulberry paper. Peel off the backing and fold ¾ inch (2cm) of the joined papers over. Repeat the process twice along the top long edge to make a strong double-folded edge to support the handles.

3 Wrap the papers around a suitable-sized box and use double-sided tape to stick the neatened side down.

4 Fold the bottom of the papers like the end of a parcel. Use double-sided tape to stick them in place.

5 Using a paper punch, punch aligning holes in the folded top edge of the bag. Cut the cord in half, and push one end of each length through a pair of holes to make a handle. Tie the ends together in a knot on the inside. Cut a piece of stiff card to fit inside the bottom of the bag and push it in place to keep the bag square.

6 Following Steps 1 and 2 of the card, stamp the white card with orange squares and spiders. Cut the squares out and use short lengths of double-sided tape to stick them to the bag.

PERSONAL STATIONERY

It is easy to make your own personalized stationery, which really can make your letters special. You will enjoy writing on these notecards almost as much as your friends will enjoy receiving them.

MATERIALS

Cosmetic sponge

Blue ink pad

Note card

Scrap paper

Clear embossing powder

Heat gun

Initial letter stamp

Corner stamp

Blue watercolor pencil

Fine paintbrush

Water

TECHNIQUES

Choosing a stamp, pages 28–31

Using ink pads, page 33

Paper and card, page 39

Positioning a single stamp, page 47

Stamping a border, page 50

Watercolor pencils, page 54

Embossing with powder, page 75

1 Dab the cosmetic sponge onto the blue ink pad and rub some color onto the right-hand edge of the note card.

2 Tip some embossing powder onto a piece of scrap paper. Dip the colored edge of the note card into it. Heat the powder until it fuses.

3 Using the blue ink pad, stamp an initial letter onto the top left-hand corner of the card.

As well as note cards, emboss the flaps of envelopes to make a coordinating set of stationery.

4 Stamp the corner design below the initial letter.

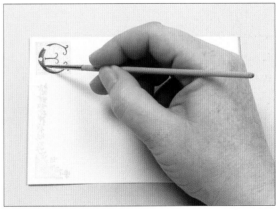

5 Color in the letter with the watercolor pencil. Dip the paintbrush into the water and carefully smooth out the color.

SOUVENIR TRAVEL JOURNAL

Make yourself a journal to take with you on your next vacation. For a special trip, in this case a honeymoon sailing holiday, personalize the journal by decorating the cover with faux postage stamps on a travel theme. Adding a luggage tag makes a perfect bookmark.

MATERIALS

Sheet of tan and buff paper

Four large travel-themed stamps

Three small complementary motif stamps

Three ink pads in different shades of brown

Watercolor pencils

Craft knife

Steel rule

Cutting mat

Gold ink pad

Printing kit

Rectangles of white paper ½ inch (1 cm) larger than finished postage stamps

Reverse-scallop decorative scissors

Spray glue

Pencil

Cosmetic sponge

Piece of map

Luggage tag

String

Metal stationary corners

All-purpose adhesive

TECHNIQUES

Choosing a stamp, pages 28–31

Using ink pads, page 33

Paper and card, page 39

Watercolor pencils, page 54

1 Stamp two travel stamps onto the tan paper and two onto the buff paper. Use two different brown inks to stamp with so that all the stamps are different. Use watercolor pencils, but no water, to color sections of the stamps in.

2 Using the craft knife and steel rule, cut the stamps into rectangles. On some of the rectangles, stamp complementary motifs in the remaining shade of brown ink.

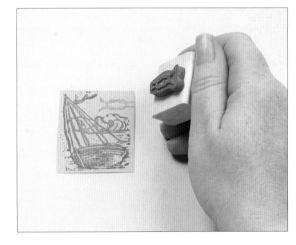

3 Make up numbers with the printing kit and, using the gold ink pad, stamp them onto the corners of the rectangles to simulate the price of the stamp.

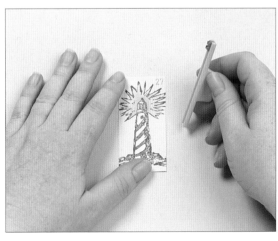

(continued)

Tie a piece of string around the front of the book to hold the book-mark down. For an added touch, finish it off with a decorative knot.

SOUVENIR TRAVEL JOURNAL *(continued)*

4 Cut around the edges of the white paper rectangles with the decorative scissors.

5 In a well-ventilated room, spray glue onto the backs of the stamped papers. Stick them centrally onto the rectangles of white paper to complete the faux postage stamps.

6 Arrange three of the stamps on the front cover of the journal. When you are happy with the placement, spray glue on the backs and stick them in position.

7 Make up the travelers' names and the date of the trip with the printing kit and an oval holder. Stamp onto the buff paper. With the stamp still in position, draw around the edge of the holder with a pencil. Lift the stamp off the paper.

8 Tear out the nameplate, following the drawn pencil line. Dab the cosmetic sponge onto the lightest brown ink pad and rub a little color around the torn edge of the nameplate.

9 Cut a piece of map to fit onto the luggage tag. Spray glue on the back of the map and stick it to the tag.

10 Using spray glue, stick the remaining postage stamp and the nameplate onto the luggage tag.

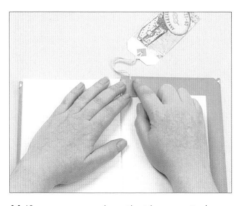

11 If necessary, replace that luggage tag's string with a longer piece. Use a piece of sticky tape to attach the end of the string to the inside back cover of the journal.

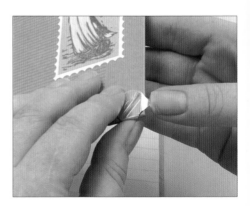

12 Finish the journal off and protect the corners by gluing a metal stationery corner to each corner of the front and back covers of the journal.

OCCASIONAL TABLE

A store-bought pine occasional table can be transformed with nostalgic, travel-themed stamps. Make this as a pleasant reminder of a special vacation, or simply as a functional furniture piece for your home. *(continued)*

Use the re-inker to tint the legs of the table to match the border around the top.

OCCASIONAL TABLE *(continued)*

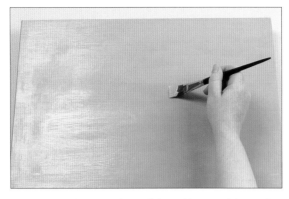

1 Paint the whole surface of the tabletop with acrylic paint. Use a wide, soft paintbrush and brush the paint on with long, smooth strokes so that the brushstroke marks don't show. Leave to dry completely.

2 Mark and tape off a 1¼-inch (3-cm) border all around the edge of the tabletop.

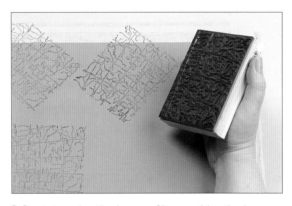

3 Start stamping the layers of images. Use the large map stamp first, and the chocolate-brown ink pad. Stamp randomly across the tabletop, allowing the stamp to go over onto the masking tape.

4 Use the large text stamp, and the chocolate-brown ink pad, to fill in the gaps.

5 Next, stamp with the travel montage stamp and the black ink pad. Use this stamp more sparingly, leaving large gaps between the images.

6 Fill in some of the gaps by stamping the luggage tags in black ink.

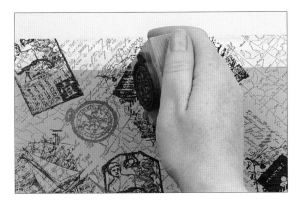

7 Finally, stamp the compass in the chocolate-brown ink, filling in any obvious gaps.

8 Peel off the masking tape very carefully. Leave all the stamps to dry completely.

9 Stick a strip of masking tape along two opposite sides of the tabletop. Stick it just inside the painted panel, covering the edges of the stamps. At the corners, lay a strip of tape at 45 degrees across the corner to create the effect of a mitered corner.

10 Using the re-inker and the wide paintbrush, paint the masked sides of the tabletop. Brush the ink on away from the tape to avoid it bleeding underneath. Leave to dry completely, then remove the tape. Mask off the remaining two sides and paint them in the same way.

11 Stick a length of masking tape just outside the stamped area all around. On two sides, run another line just inside the first one so that the edge of the stamped panel lies in the gap between the two lengths of tape.

12 Draw over the gap and edges of tape with a gold-leaf pen. Remove the tape and leave to dry. Mask off the inside edges of the remaining two sides and repeat the process. If any of the gold bleeds, touch it up afterward. Seal the tabletop with two coats of matte varnish.

RETRO PICTURE FRAME

Revisit the 1920s with this retro-style picture frame. Simple and elegant, it's a perfect complement for either black-and-white or color photograph.

MATERIALS

Four sheets of mulberry paper in different pastel colors

Selection of 1920s-style stamps. One should be a small-scale background image, and the others larger-scale images

Embossing ink pad

Gold embossing powder

Heat gun

Fine paintbrush

Water

Gold picture frame

Soft paintbrush

PVA craft glue

TECHNIQUES

Choosing a stamp, page 28–31

Embossing with powder, page 75

This frame could also be made using distinctive designs from a different era, such as the 1950s.

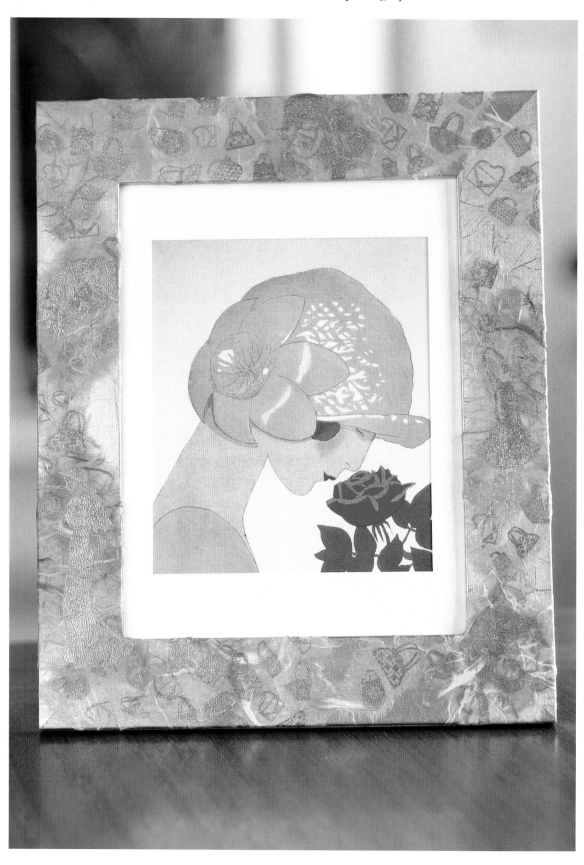

1 Emboss all the sheets of mulberry paper with the stamps in gold embossing powder. Do not confine one stamp to one color of paper; stamp with all of them onto all the papers.

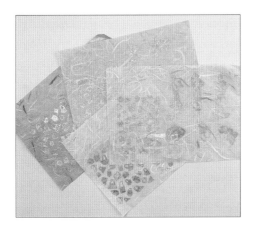

2 Dip the paintbrush into water and brush around each stamp. Keep dipping the paintbrush into the water so that the line on the paper is well dampened.

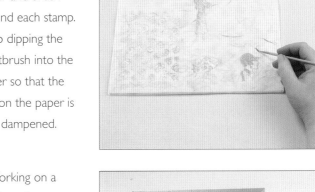

3 Pull along the dampened line to tear out each stamp. Where the long fibers cross the wet line, ease them out of the paper. Tear out each stamp in this way.

4 Working on a small section at a time, brush some craft glue onto the picture frame.

5 Lay a torn-out background stamp onto the glued section and brush over it with a little more glue. Don't worry that it looks white at this stage; the glue will be clear when dry.

6 Continue building up the background in this way. Do not cover all of the frame; some of the gold should show through. Leave the frame to dry.

7 Again working on a small section at a time, brush some glue over the background. Position a larger-scaled stamp on the glued section, and brush over it with a little more glue.

8 Continue pasting stamps until the frame looks well balanced.

WEDDING INVITATION

Making your own wedding invitations not only adds a very personal touch to one of life's major moments but it can also save you a lot of money. However, getting the balance between something that is pretty and doesn't take forever to do, can be tricky. This invitation is deceptively quick to make and looks stunning, too.

MATERIALS

Frame stamp

Gold ink pad

Pale pink mulberry paper

Steel rule

Craft knife

Cutting mat

Spray glue

Card blanks

Heart stamp

Cream card

Gold embossing powder

Heat gun

Self-adhesive pads

Sheets with printed wedding details (see panel)

Variegated pink embroidery thread

Small beads

TECHNIQUES

Choosing a stamp, page 28–31

Using ink pads, page 33

Paper and card, page 39

Embossing with powder, page 75

Consider making other elements of wedding stationery to match the invitations—menus, church programs, and place cards.

1 Using the gold ink pad, stamp the number of frames you need onto the pale pink paper. Leave them to dry.

2 Using the steel rule and craft knife, cut the frames out. Cut just outside the stamped design so that there is a border of paper around the frame.

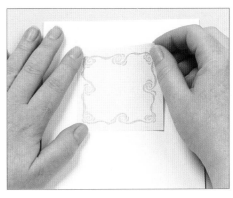

3 In a well-ventilated room, spray glue onto the back of each frame and stick one onto the face of each card blank.

4 Stamp as many hearts as you need onto the cream card with gold ink. Stamp them in evenly spaced rows. Emboss them with gold embossing powder.

5 Lay the steel rule between two rows of hearts and carefully tear along it. Tear the card between every row, and then between every heart, until they are all torn out.

6 Stick a self-adhesive pad onto the back of each heart and stick one into the middle of each frame.

PRINTING THE WEDDING DETAILS
Choose a paper size that will fit neatly into the card blanks once it is folded in half. Use a computer to write out the details, then either print them out or have them copied. Remember that you will need to arrange the details on the page so that they appear on the right-hand side once the paper is folded.

7 Fold the sheets with the wedding details and slide one into each card.

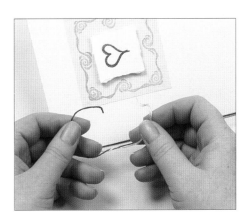

8 Tie a length of embroidery thread around the spine of each card to hold the sheet in place. Thread a bead onto each end of the thread and tie a knot to hold it in place. Trim the ends of the thread.

SNOWY SCRAPBOOK PAGE

Stamps can be used to make the most beautiful scrapbook pages. Using one motif on a variety of different surfaces keeps the whole page looking fresh and gives the photographs maximum impact.

MATERIALS

Two photographs

Pale pink paper

Steel rule

Craft knife

Cutting mat

Double-sided tape

Photocopy acetate

Opalescent paper

Large, medium, and small snowflake stamps

White stamp pad

Crystal sparkle embossing powder

Piece of dense foam

Dressmaker's pin

Blue vellum

Clear embossing ink pad

White sparkle embossing powder

Four cream mini-eyelets and fixing tool

Sheet of thick cream paper

Sharp scissors

Invisible thread

Small glass beads

TECHNIQUES

Choosing a stamp, page 28–31

Using ink pads, page 33

Paper and card, page 39

Positioning a single stamp, page 47

Embossing with powder, page 75

Personalize your own page with a flower stamp for summer pictures or a heart for wedding photographs.

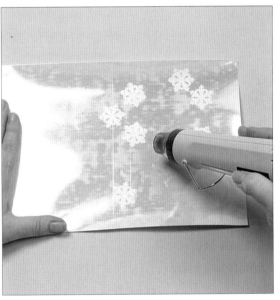

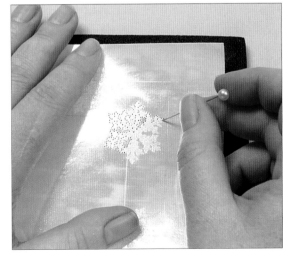

1 Cut an aperture in the pink paper large enough to accommodate one of your photographs. Stick double-sided tape around the aperture and stick a piece of acetate over it.

2 On the opalescent paper, mark out a frame large enough to surround your other photograph. Emboss some medium snowflakes onto the frame, allowing some of them to overlap both the inner and outer edges of the frame. Use the white stamp pad and crystal sparkle embossing powder.

3 Position a snowflake over the foam and, using the pin, pierce holes around the edges of the snowflake. Repeat the process on all the snowflakes.

(continued)

4 Using a craft knife and steel rule, cut out the frame. Where the snowflakes protrude over the border, carefully cut freehand along the lines of piercing.

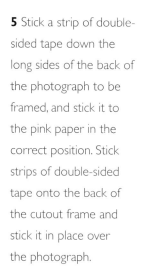

5 Stick a strip of double-sided tape down the long sides of the back of the photograph to be framed, and stick it to the pink paper in the correct position. Stick strips of double-sided tape onto the back of the cutout frame and stick it in place over the photograph.

6 Tear a strip of blue vellum the same length as the pink paper. Stick a strip of double-sided tape down the back of the left-hand side of the pink paper. Stick the blue vellum to this so that a narrow strip of it protrudes on the left-hand side of the pink paper.

7 Place the other picture behind the piece of acetate. Using the clear pad, stamp a drift of small snowflakes across the acetate, positioning them sensitively over the photograph. Continue the drift across the pink paper and onto the blue vellum.

Remove the photograph and emboss the stamps with the white sparkle powder. Be especially careful to brush away any stray flecks of embossing powder on the acetate before heating it. Use double-sided tape to stick the photograph behind the acetate.

8 Use the eyelets to fasten the pink paper to the cream paper. Center the pink paper on the cream paper and position one eyelet at each corner of the pink paper.

9 Using the white ink pad and crystal sparkle powder, emboss one large and one medium snowflake onto acetate. Cut them out with sharp scissors. Thread the snowflakes onto a long length of invisible thread, threading on a few glass beads above, below, and in between them. Tie one end of the thread to the top right eyelet and the other end to the bottom right eyelet, pulling the thread quite taut between them.

MOSAIC FLOORCLOTH

This is a very simple project to make, and it will look fresh and colorful in a child's bedroom. The secret to success is choosing a harmonious set of paint colors and keeping them balanced across the floorcloth so that one color does not dominate the whole project. Stand back from your work occasionally to check that it is progressing along these lines.

MATERIALS

Six paint pads

Four light-colored fabric paints

Four square, textured stamps

Plain canvas floorcloth

Two strong-colored fabric paints

Spiral stamp

TECHNIQUES

Choosing a stamp, pages 28–31

Making a paint pad, page 36

Stamping with fabric paints, page 71

Shadow stamping, page 83

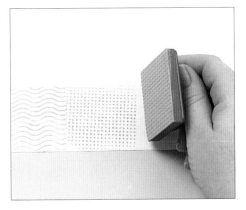

1 Make a paint pad for each light-colored paint. Dab one textured stamp onto each color pad. Start stamping the mosaic along one long side of the floorcloth, alternating the colors. If the stamps overlap one end of the floorcloth, don't worry; it won't spoil the finished look. Butt the stamps up against one another so that as little as possible of the canvas is showing.

Colorful and simple, the perfect project for any child's bedroom.

2 Continue stamping the mosaic, working up and across the cloth. Keep standing back from it to check that you are maintaining a good balance of the four different colors. When you have completed the mosaic, leave it to dry completely.

3 Make a paint pad for each strong-colored paint. Dab the spiral onto one color pad. Stamp some spirals onto the floorcloth, positioning them sensitively on the mosaic background. Clean the stamp.

4 Dab the stamp onto the other color pad and stamp some more spirals. Ensure that you keep the colors and patterns well balanced. Iron the back of the canvas to fix the colors.

VICTORIAN-STYLE STATIONERY

Handwritten letters can be made extra special by using paper decorated in a Victorian style. Make envelopes to match, and even the mailman will stop to admire your letter.

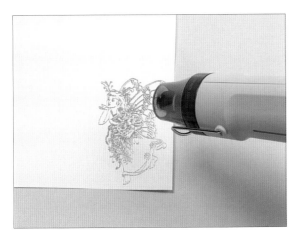

1 Using the gold ink pad and embossing powder, stamp and emboss the fairy onto the bottom right-hand corner of the sheet of paper.

2 Next, stamp and emboss the corner design. Align the edges of the stamp backing with the corner of the paper.

3 Finally, stamp the border designs, spacing them evenly along the edges of the paper.

4 Using the watercolor pens and water method, color in the fairy. Use leaf green for the wings and dress, pink and crimson for the flowers, and brown for the hair.

5 Color in the corner and border designs to complement the fairy.

Emboss envelopes to match the writing paper, but do not color them in—if they get damp the color will run.

MATERIALS

Writing paper and envelopes

Gold ink pad

Gold embossing powder

Heat gun

Rose flower fairy stamp

Rose and trellis corner stamp

Rose border stamp

Rose pink, crimson, leaf green and dark brown watercolor pens

Fine paintbrush

Water

TECHNIQUES

Choosing a stamp, page 28–31

Paper and card, page 39

Positioning a single stamp, page 47

Stamping a border, page 50

Watercolor pens, page 53

Embossing with powder, page 75

WATERCOLOR PAINTING

Pretty and feminine, this watercolor picture is a work of art. However, you don't need to be very artistic to make it—simple stamping and punching techniques will do most of the work for you.

1 Color the flower stamp with the purple and yellow pens. Make the petals purple and the center yellow.

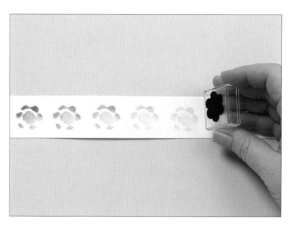

2 Stamp a strip of watercolor paper with flowers. Re-color the stamp every second or third time to produce stronger and paler flowers.

3 Using a fine paintbrush and water, smudge the colors to create a watercolor effect. Leave to dry.

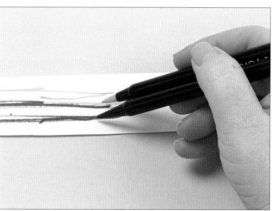

4 Turn the strip over and scribble on the back of it with the purple and yellow pens.

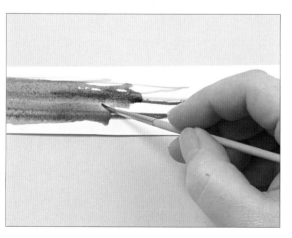

5 Again using the paintbrush and water, blend the colors over the whole strip of paper.

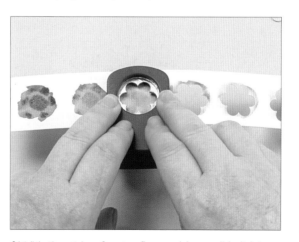

6 With the strip of paper flower-side up, slide it into the punch until a flower is visible. Punch out the flower. Punch out all the flowers on the strip.

(continued)

MATERIALS

Small punched flower stamp

Purple, yellow, and green watercolor pens

Strips of watercolor paper

Fine paintbrush

Water

Small flower punch

Foam mat

Butterfly and leaf punched stamps and punches

Piece of watercolor paper to fit picture frame

Block stamp

Pale purple, green, yellow, and pink ink pads

Silicone glue

Picture frame

TECHNIQUES

Punched stamp, page 24

Using ink pads, page 33

Using brush pens, page 34

Paper and card, page 39

Watercolor pens, page 53

Stamping and punching, page 81

Shadow stamping, page 83

Color the picture to suit your room or to reflect your own favorite flowers.

WATERCOLOR PAINTING *(continued)*

7 Lay a flower on the foam mat and press into the center of it with the end of a pen. The petals will naturally curl up. Treat all of the flowers in this way.

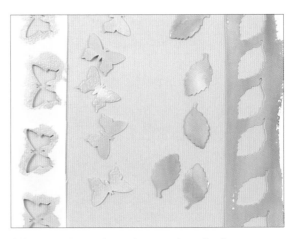

8 Stamp, color, and punch out strips of yellow butterflies and green leaves. They do not need to be colored on the backs.

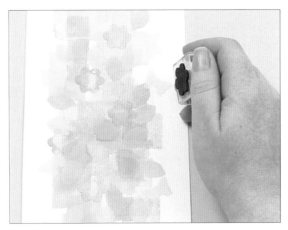

9 Shadow stamp the large piece of watercolor paper. Make a dense background of blocks, flowers, butterflies, and leaves. Leave to dry.

10 Put a dot of silicone glue on the back of each flower and stick it to the background. Position the flowers randomly.

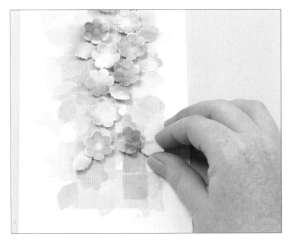

11 Apply a little glue to the stalk end of each leaf and stick them on. Tuck the glued end under the petals of the flowers.

12 Finally, stick on the butterflies, sticking some to the background and some onto the flowers. Fit the picture into the frame.

MEMORY BOX

Stamped with pink hearts and finished with organza ribbon, this romantic project will keep precious love letters safe in their very own memory box for years to come.   *(continued)*

This box is all about love, but you could use the same techniques to make a box for holiday cards, letters from friends, or baby mementoes.

MEMORY BOX *(continued)*

MATERIALS

Wooden box painted pink

Cosmetic sponge

Metallic pink ink pad

Rectangle of pink paper the size of the box lid

Scallop-edged decorative scissors

Piece of dense foam

Dressmaker's pin

Spray glue

Four different small heart stamps

Torn strips of handmade paper the length and depth of the box lid sides

Two different pink ink pads

One brown ink pad

Rectangle of handmade paper ½ inch (1 cm) smaller all around than the box lid

Double-curl stamp

Three-dimensional silver paint

Double-sided tape

Two pieces of organza ribbon

TECHNIQUES

Choosing a stamp, page 28–31

Using ink pads, page 33

Paper and card, page 39

Positioning a single stamp, page 47

Using three-dimensional paints, page 76

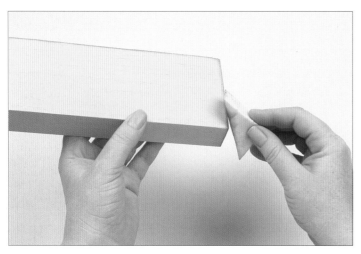

1 Dab the cosmetic sponge onto the metallic pink ink pad and rub some color onto the edges of the box lid. Leave it to dry.

2 Using the heart stamps and all the inks, stamp rows of hearts onto the narrow strips of handmade paper.

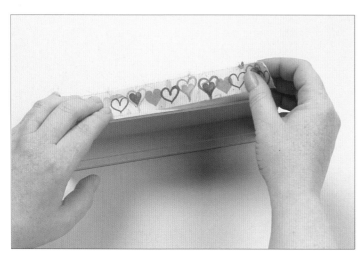

3 In a well-ventilated room, use spray glue to stick one strip to each edge of the box lid.

4 Trim the edges of the pink paper with the decorative scissors.

5 Lay the paper on the foam and use the pin to pierce a pattern of decorative holes along the cut edge.

6 Spray glue on the back of the paper and stick it centrally to the top of the box.

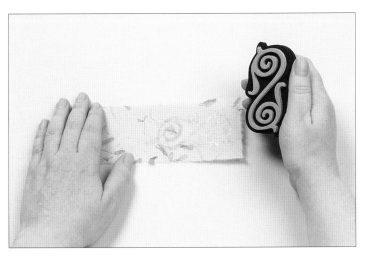

7 Using the metallic pink ink pad, stamp the larger piece of handmade paper with the double-curl stamp.

8 Using spray glue, stick the paper centrally to the lid of the box.

9 Use the three-dimensional paint to highlight areas of the stamp.

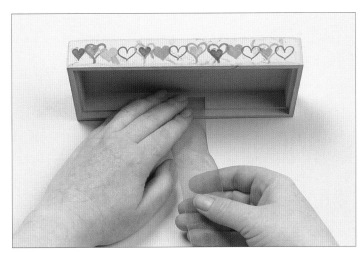

10 Stick a small piece of double-sided tape to one end of each piece of ribbon and stick them to the opposite inner side of the lid. Tie them in a bow on top of the lid.

TEDDY BEAR PLACE CARDS

Make a child's birthday extra special by creating name cards for the children coming to the party. At the end of the day, attach the cards to party favors for the children to take home.

MATERIALS

Steel rule

Pencil

Piece of cream card, the width and twice the length of the finished place card

Teddy bear stamp

Stamp positioner

Chocolate-brown ink pad

Clear embossing powder

Heat gun

Craft knife

Cutting mat

Light and dark brown watercolor pens

Plate

Fine paintbrush

Water

Gold leaf pen

Scrap paper

Small piece of cream card for name

Gold sticky letters

Paper adhesive

TECHNIQUES

Choosing a stamp, page 28–31

Paper and card, page 39

Positioning a single stamp, page 47

Stamping a border, page 50

Watercolor pens, page 53

1 Make a tiny pencil mark on each long edge of the piece of card, halfway up. Stamp two teddy bears onto the card, positioning them so that their heads overlap the halfway mark. Stamp the bears in chocolate-brown ink, then sprinkle clear embossing powder over them and emboss them.

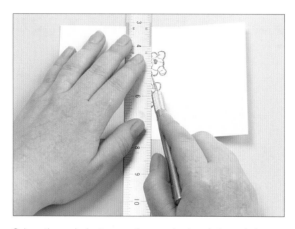

2 Lay the rule between the marked points and draw along it with the back of the craft knife to create a score line. Do not draw across the stamped bears, and do not fold the card.

3 Carefully cut around the parts of the bears' heads that protrude above the score line. Fold the card in half, allowing the heads to pop up.

4 Lay the card flat again and stamp three bears in a row along the bottom edge.

5 Scribble some light brown watercolor pen onto a small plate. Dip a fine paintbrush in water and dilute the color a little. Paint the bears, apart from their muzzles. Dilute a little ink from a dark brown pen and use this to color the bears' muzzles, and to add a little shading to their arms and legs.

6 Use a gold leaf pen to draw a border around three sides of the card front. To draw a straight line, turn the card so that the edge you are working on is horizontal, and lay it on a piece of scrap paper. Place the pen at one end, with the nib positioned half on the card and half on the scrap paper; following the edge of the card will help you keep the line straight. In one continuous line, draw right across the edge of the card. Repeat the process on each edge.

7 Lay a piece of scrap paper across the bottom of the name card and use this as a guide for sticking down the name. Align the bottom of each sticky letter with the top of the paper so that they all sit in a straight line. Draw a border around the name card in the same way as in Step 5.

8 Using paper adhesive, stick the name card to the center front of the main card.

These perky bears are perfect for a children's party, but you could use the same idea, with an appropriate stamp, to make name cards for any type of party.

SILVER PENDANT

Similar in texture and feel to polymer clay, precious metal clay is wonderful stuff. It contains pure silver, and when you heat it, the carrying medium is burned away and you are left with a piece of silver. This clay can be bought in kit form with the butane torch, fireproof block, wire brush, and full instructions.

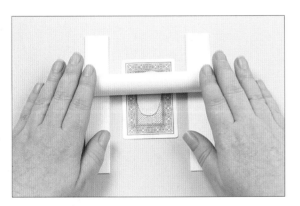

2 Roll out the clay so the pin touches the plastic guides.

4 Using the craft knife, cut out the pendant shape.

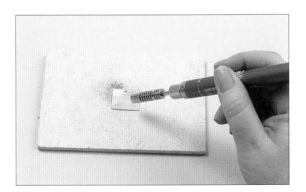

6 Following the manufacturer's instructions carefully, place the pendant on the fireproof block and heat it until it glows. Leave it to cool completely.

3 Stamp into the clay, pressing gently.

5 Use the pointed tool to make a hole to hang the pendant from. Leave it to dry.

7 Use the wire brush to remove the white residue on the surface of the pendant, revealing the shining silver.

1 Lay the playing card on a flat surface and rub a little vegetable oil onto it to stop the clay sticking. Position a piece of plastic on either side of it; these will act as depth guides when you are rolling out the clay.

MATERIALS

Precious metal clay

Playing card

Vegetable oil

Two pieces of 1/16-inch- (2-mm-) thick plastic

Tiny rolling pin or bottle

small leaf stamp

Craft knife

Pointed tool

fireproof block

Butane torch

Wire brush

TECHNIQUES

Choosing a stamp, pages 28–31

Stamping onto polymer clay, page 78

Create a collection of jewelry, including a bracelet and earrings, to match the pendant.

MOTIF LIBRARY

Animals

**Animals
(continued)**

Birds

Birds
(continued)

Seashore

Flora

Flora (continued)

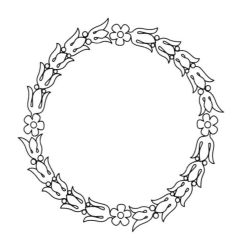

Flora (continued)

Flora (continued)

Miscellaneous Motifs

Panels

Panels (continued)

Patterns

Borders, Frames, and Banners

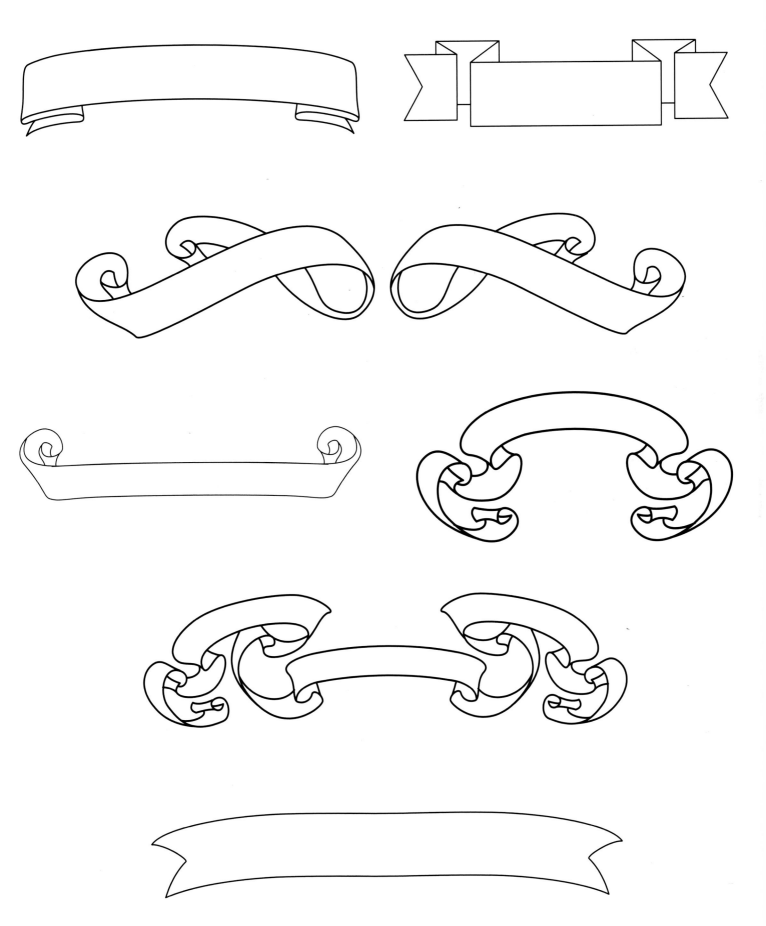

Borders, Frames, and Banners (continued)

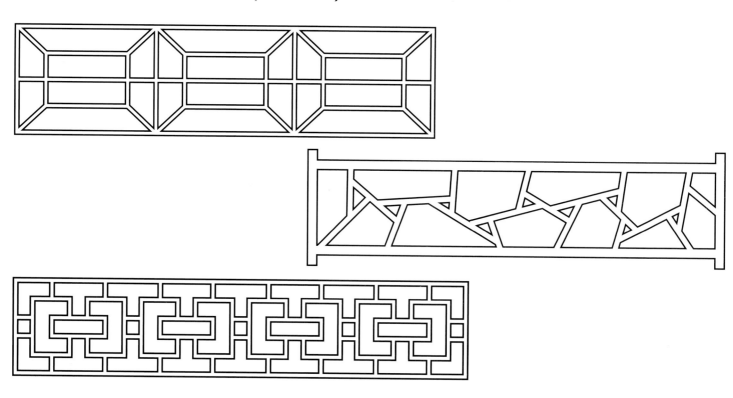

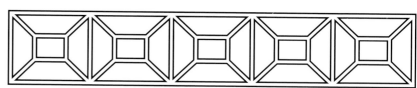

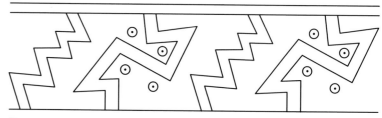

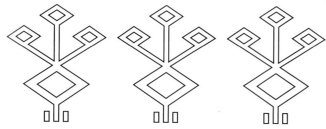

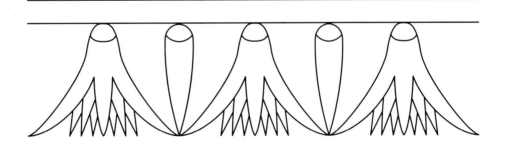

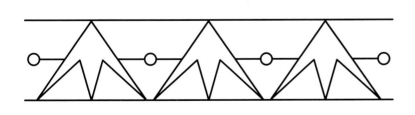

Borders, Frames, and Banners (continued)

Letters and Numbers

A B C D E F G

H I J K L M N

O P Q R S T U

V W X Y Z

1 2 3 4 5 6 7 8 9 0

SUPPLIERS

UK

Rainbow Glass
85 Walkden Road, Worsley
Manchester M28 7BQ
Tel: 0161 790 3025
Fax: 0161 661 5787
www.rainbowglass.com
info@rainbowglass.com
Glass outliner, self adhesive rubber sheets, self adhesive films, thick film, double sided self adhesive film and rubber stamping accessories.

The Stamp Craft Studio
11 The Arcade
Letchworth Garden City
Hertfordshire SG6 3ET
Tel 01462 681551
Fax 01462 811732
www.thestampcraftstudio.com
info@thestampcraftstudio.com
Creative inspiration for rubber stamping, scrapbooking and card making projects. Regular workshops for all ages and abilities, party plans, gift vouchers, wedding and party stationery kits. Visit or contact us for mail order information.

Ideal World TV
Newark Road
Peterborough PE1 5WG
Tel: 08700 700800 (order line)
www.createandcraft.tv
Complete range of craft products covering every aspect of crafting. Ideal World on digital satellite 635 or NTL digital 855.

Create & Craft TV
Newark Road
Peterborough, PE1 5WG
Tel: 08700 700300 (order line)
www.createandcraft.tv
Complete range of craft products covering every aspect of crafting. Craft programmes 24 hours a day on digital satellite 695 or can be viewed on the website.

Hobbycraft
Call 0800-0272387 for your nearest store.
Art and craft superstore.

Personal Impressions
Curzon Road
Chiltern Industrial Estate
Sudbury
Suffolk CO10 2XW
Tel: 01787 375241
Fax: 01787 310179
sales @Richstamp.co.uk
www.Richstamp.co.uk
Rubber stamps and materials.

Woodware Toys & Gifts BV
Unit 2A Sandylands Business Park, Skipton
North Yorkshire BD23 2DE
Tel: 01756 700024
Fax: 01756 701097
Rubber stamps and materials.
The Cutting Edge
Unit 17a, CEC, Mill Lane,
Coppull, Lancashire PR7 5BW
Tel: 01257-792025
sales@eco-craft.co.uk
www.eco-craft.co.uk
Stamps, materials and papers.

Royal Brush Manufacturing (UK) Ltd
Block 3, Unit 3
Wednesbury Trading Estate
Bliston Road, Wednesbury
West Midlands WS10 7JN
Tel: 0121 556 8422
Fax: 0121 556 9968
uk@royalbrush.com
www.royalbrush.com
Wet and grow sponges, scraper boards, stencil brushes, paint brushes and general craft suppliers. Call for stockists.

Stampeezee
349 Walsgrave Road, Ball Hill
Coventry CV2 4BE
Tel: 024-7644 80 85
Stamping supplies.

Craft Creations
Ingersoll House
Delamare Road, Cheshunt
Hertfordshire EN8 9HD
Tel: 01922-781 900
enquiries@craftcreations.com
www.craftcreations.com
Craft materials.

Express Services
Vernon Court , Henson Way
Telford Way Industrial Estate
Kettering
Northants NN16 8PX
Tel: 01536 481778
Fax: 01536 521412
www.express-services.uk.com
Layered stamps, embossing powders, glitters and stamping accessories.

Graphicus
Fountains Court
High Etherley
Bishop Auckland
Co Durham DL14 0LZ
Tel: 01388 834 934
Fax: 01388 830 919
www.graphicus.co.uk
info@graphicus.co.uk
Layered stamps, embossing powders, glitters and stamping accessories.

The English Stamp Company
Worth Matravers
Dorset BH19 3JP
Tel: 01929 439117
Fax: 01929 439150
www.englishstamp.com
sales@englishstamp.com
Stamps, ink pads, embossing powders, roller stamps and general stamping accessories.

Silver Alchemy Marketing Ltd
2 Marshall St
London W1F 9BB
08707 517 607 order line
08707 517 608 fax
info@silveralchemy.com
www.silveralchemy.com
Precious metal clay

Cakeboards
George Street, Burnley
Lancs BB11 1LX
Tel: 01282 423142
Fax:01282 477048
www.cakeboards.co.uk
Sugar paste, edible ink pens, lustre powders and food colouring.

Barking Dog
Merchant House
Market Street
Rugby, CV21 3HF
Tel: 01788 556900
Fax: 01788 556910
sales@barkingdogcraft.co.uk
www.barkingdogcraft.co.uk
Blank cards, envelopes, acetate and comprehensive range of card making products.

Hero Arts Rubber Stamps Inc.
1343 Powell Street
Emeryville, California 94608
www.heroarts.com

Personal Stamp Exchange (PSX)
360 Sutton Place
Santa Rosa
CA 95407
Tel;1 800 7826748
Fax:1 800 7793297
www.psxdesign.com
info@psxdesign.com
Personal Impressions and Woodware are the UK distributors for PSX stamps.

Stampendous
1240 North Red Gum
Anaheim, CA 92806-1820
Tel: 1 800 869 0474
www.spampendous.com
stamp@stampendous.com
Woodware is the UK distributor for Stampendous.

INDEX

ACKNOWLEDGMENTS

Alan D Gear and Barry L Freestone would like to thank Sarah Beaman and Teresa Philpott for the wonderful work they have done for this book. They would also like to thank Kate Haxell for editing the book, Matt Dickens for photographing it, Roger Daniels for designing it, and Collins & Brown for commissioning it.

Alan and Barry can be contacted through rainbowglass@aol.com

Teresa Philpott can be contacted at info@thestampcraftstudio.com

Sarah Beaman can be contacted at sarah.beaman1@btopenworld.com